Educating Children with Complex Conditions

Downloadable Material

If you go to http://www.sagepub.co.uk/dittrich you will be able to download PDFs of the photocopiable material included in this book.

Educating Children with Complex Conditions

Understanding overlapping and co-existing developmental disorders

Winand H. Dittrich and Rona Tutt

Los Angeles • London • New Delhi • Singapore • Washington DC

SAGE Publications Ltd
1 Oliver's Yard
55 City Road
London EC1Y 1SP

SAGE Publications Inc.
2455 Teller Road
Thousand Oaks, California 91320

SAGE Publications India Pvt Ltd
B 1/I 1 Mohan Cooperative Industrial Area
Mathura Road
New Delhi 110 044

SAGE Publications Asia-Pacific Pte Ltd
33 Pekin Street #02-01
Far East Square
Singapore 048763

Library of Congress Control Number 2008923544

British Library Cataloguing in Publication data

A catalogue record for this book is available from the British Library

ISBN 978-1-84787-317-0
ISBN 978-1-84787-318-7 (pbk)

Typeset by C&M Digitals (P) Ltd, Chennai, India
Printed in Great Britain by the Cromwell Press, Trowbridge, Wiltshire
Printed on paper from sustainable resources

Dedication

This book is dedicated to children and young people who have developmental disorders, the families who support them, the schools who educate them, and the neuropsychologists and other professionals who try to unearth the nature of their difficulties. Also to those involved in initial teacher training or continuing professional development, who are helping to ensure that there are closer links between researchers and those whose work has a direct effect on children with complex conditions.

The Association for all School Leaders

With a membership of over 28,000, the National Association of Head Teachers is the largest organisation of its kind in Europe. Representing headteachers, principals, deputies, vice-principals and assistant headteachers, it has provided over a century of dedicated support to its members. The union speaks with authority and strength on educational issues covering early years, primary, secondary and special sectors.

National Association of Head Teachers
1 Heath Square, Boltro Road, Haywards Heath, West Sussex, RH16 1BL
Tel: +44(0) 1444 472472; email: info@naht.org.uk; website: www.naht.org.uk

Contents

About the authors

The authors of this book are listed in alphabetical order as they shared equal responsibility for writing it.

Winand H. Dittrich is a Reader in Experimental Psychology at the University of Hertfordshire. His main research interests are in cognitive neuropsychology and the workings of the human mind. He was one of the first researchers to make a systematic study of the damaging effects of neurotropic viruses (similar to HIV or BSE) on brain functions in 1989. He has published empirical studies on attention, working memory and movement control in Parkinson's disease, on the perception of human movement and emotional dance displays, on the recognition of facial expressions in adults, the elderly and children with autistic spectrum disorders. He has proposed a new theoretical framework for movement perception in animal as well as human vision. Together with colleagues, he has extended the understanding of the cognitive control of simple motor skills in healthy and brain-damaged people. His theoretical approach has been applied in sport and exercise sciences as well as in medical sciences. Recently, he co-developed a new diagnostic instrument to evaluate the neuropsychological profile of obsessions and compulsions in anxiety disorders. Several of his research papers on diverse topics have been cited over 100 times.

Winand enjoys the challenges of teaching students of all abilities and from diverse backgrounds, particularly those who, until a few years ago, would have had no opportunity to develop their educational achievements at such a level.

Rona Tutt has taught children with SEN in state and independent, residential and day, mainstream and special schools. Trained originally as a teacher of the deaf, she became the head teacher of Woolgrove School in Hertfordshire, a school for pupils who have moderate learning difficulties. She established the local authority's first provision for pupils with autistic spectrum disorders within the school. In 2003, Rona was the winner of the Leadership in Teaching Award. In 2004, she received an OBE for her services to special needs education. From 2004 to 2005, she was President of the National Association for Head Teachers. She continues to work for them as a SEN consultant.

Rona writes on a number of educational issues and is much in demand as a speaker. In 2007, her first book, *Every Child Included*, was published, which looks beyond the inclusion debate to illustrate, by means of case studies of schools, the range of provision that is developing. The book also looks at how schools are addressing the Every Child Matters (ECM) agenda alongside their provision for SEN.

Rona is Chair of Governors at Heathlands School in St Albans, which caters for severely and profoundly deaf children, and Vice Chair of Governors at The Valley School in Stevenage, which is for secondary pupils with MLD and ASD.

Acknowledgements

The authors would like to offer their sincere thanks to:

Professor Stuart Powell for introducing the authors to each other;

The University of Hertfordshire for enabling the necessary research to take place;

Professor Wendy Purcell for her encouragement to pursue this interdisciplinary research;

The National Association for Special Educational Needs (Nasen) for their support;

Mirko Schuessler, a visiting placement student from the University Duisburg-Essen for his illustrations of the brain and his assistance with research.

How to use this book

This book is designed to help those who are leading schools or working with children who have complex conditions to:

- become more familiar with what is meant by overlapping and co-existing disorders

- increase their understanding of the links between how the brain works and how children learn

- use this knowledge to develop ways of teaching that will help all pupils and particularly those who have difficulties to overcome

- consider other factors that can impinge on learning, including nutrition and the use of therapists

- take a holistic view in order to provide the best possible support to the child

- look at what more needs to be done to improve that support in the future.

The layout of each chapter is similar, and includes:

- a list of what will be covered, at the beginning of the chapter

- key points that are highlighted where appropriate

- questions for reflection to make the book more interactive, and to serve as the basis for discussion and debate elsewhere

- key terms, described in the glossary, are written in bold

- a summary at the end.

In addition, some of the pages are photocopiable in order to provide resources that can be used to record the nature of a pupil's difficulties, their progress over time, and strategies for meeting their needs.

Although some readers may prefer to turn to particular chapters first, most will be gained from reading through the book from the start, as each chapter builds on the preceding ones.

The first chapter gives an overview of a group of four developmental disorders which have been selected because they are becoming increasingly common, have overlapping symptoms and links in the form of co-existence. This is followed by a chapter on the workings of the brain in relation to neurological disorders. The third chapter considers diagnostic labels and how far they are useful. The next chapter moves on to focusing on how the information gathered so far can be translated into helping pupils in the classroom. The penultimate chapter looks at what part non-pedagogical approaches should play in helping to ameliorate pupils' difficulties, including nutrition and the role of other professionals. The final chapter pulls together the threads that have been running through the book, ties these in with some of the current developments in schools, and makes suggestions as to what should happen in future to meet more effectively the needs of an increasingly complex population of pupils to be found in today's classroom.

1

Defining overlapping and co-existing conditions

This chapter sets the scene for the rest of the book by:

- presenting case studies of two children as illustrations of overlapping and co-existing disorders
- explaining how the terms used to describe childhood disorders have changed over time
- discussing the meaning of overlapping disorders and ones that co-exist
- defining the four main groupings of developmental disorders that are the focus of this book.

What's in a label?

It is a comparatively recent phenomenon that children with **developmental disorders** may be given not just one diagnosis but two or more. This has happened at a time when the number of terms being used to describe different disorders has increased. For instance, '**specific learning difficulties**' now covers not just **dyslexia**, but **dyspraxia**, **dyscalculia** and **dysgraphia** as well. Other terms, such as **autism**, have broadened their definition to become '**autistic spectrum disorders**' (ASD), which includes **Asperger's syndrome**. As the numbers of **labels** being used have both increased and expanded, it has become apparent that children with different disorders may exhibit some of the same symptoms. It has also become clear that there are certain conditions that quite often go together, so that what were once seen as entirely separate disorders now need to be viewed as ones that may overlap or co-exist. The question then arises as to how to educate these more complex children, while not detracting from the educational experiences of their peers. This book has been written to shed light on the current situation, to consider the impact of certain conditions on children's ability to learn effectively, and to look at the approaches and strategies that might assist all children to become successful learners.

Case study 1.1: Tommy, 8 years old

Tommy was seven years old when he received a diagnosis of attention deficit hyperactivity disorder (ADHD) from the family doctor. He had struggled to cope in his infant school, and the staff had struggled to cope with his behaviour, which combined impulsiveness with an inability to concentrate on anything for more than a few minutes. As he moved to his junior school and the same pattern of behaviour continued, his parents agreed with the doctor that it would be worth putting him on medication for a trial period. Unfortunately, this seemed to have little effect, so after a few months the medication was stopped. Tommy's behaviour continued to be erratic. When he was eight, and after being involved in several playground fights, the school excluded him for lashing out at a member of staff who was trying to direct him to go back to class at the end of playtime.

On his return to school after his fixed-term exclusion, he was seen by the school's educational psychologist (EP), who sent him to a paediatrician. After assessing Tommy, the paediatrician explained to his parents that their son met the criteria for a diagnosis of Asperger's syndrome and that ASD would be a more accurate description of Tommy's difficulties than ADHD.

Case study 1.2: Sylvie, 12 years old

Sylvie had been diagnosed with dyslexia when she was eight years old. Her teachers had always expressed surprise that someone who was so keen to do well had struggled to get off the ground with both reading and written work. Not only was her spelling very weak, but her handwriting was almost illegible. For the rest of her time in primary school, Sylvie received extra help twice a week from a teaching assistant who worked with a small group and concentrated on improving the pupils' reading ability. Although Sylvie made some progress, as the gap between her and her peers widened, she became less motivated and her behaviour deteriorated. She also found it hard to make friends and was often the last one to be picked for team games, mainly because she was slow at running and her ball skills were poor.

When she reached secondary school, Sylvie was placed in the learning support unit (LSU), where the teacher in charge decided to look more closely at the nature of her difficulties. From the assessments the teacher carried out in conjunction with a specialist teacher for dyslexia, there seemed to be no doubt that Sylvie had severe dyslexia. However, in addition, she was referred to the local child development centre, where her difficulties with coordination resulted in the physiotherapist and the occupational therapist agreeing that she had dyspraxia in addition to her dyslexia.

In the first of these case studies, Tommy begins by having a diagnosis of ADHD, which is later replaced by one of ASD. This is an example where a label is changed over the course of time, as the child's development seems to indicate that a different term might be a more accurate one. At first glance, it may seem that ADHD and ASD are two very different conditions; yet, children with either condition can appear to be inattentive and socially inept. In Tommy's case, as he grew older, one label was changed for the other; in other cases, a child may be diagnosed with both ADHD *and* ASD.

The second case study is that of a child who acquires the label 'dyslexia' and it is later discovered that she also has another specific learning difficulty in the form of dyspraxia. In this case, the first label was not wrong, but it may have prevented professionals working with her from realising that dyslexia was not her only difficulty. In Sylvie's case, it was not so much a question of overlapping symptoms (although, as discussed later in this chapter, all four of the specific learning difficulties recognised to date do have some symptoms in common), but that specific learning difficulties can co-exist. Later on, it will become apparent that they can also co-exist with some of the other disorders explored in this book.

At first glance, it may seem that there is a clear distinction between the terms *overlapping* and *co-existing* disorders.

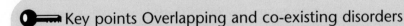

Key points Overlapping and co-existing disorders

Overlapping disorders

Overlapping disorders are ones that have some symptoms in common (as in the case of Tommy in Case Study 1.1).

Co-existing disorders/co-morbidity

Co-existing disorders or co-morbidity is the term used when the same child has more than one condition (as in the case of Sylvie in Case Study 1.2).

Note: The terms *condition* and *disorder* are used interchangeably in this book.

However, there may come a point when two conditions that are seen as overlapping, share so many symptoms, that it is no longer sensible to talk of them as being separate disorders. For instance, time will tell whether or not dysgraphia will establish itself as being sufficiently different from dyslexia, or whether the definition of dyslexia will broaden to encompass dysgraphia. (The four types of specific learning difficulties are described later in this chapter.)

Questions for reflection

1. Can you think of a child you know who was diagnosed with one condition, which was subsequently changed to a different diagnosis?

2. Do you know of any children who have been diagnosed with more than one condition?

3. Can you think of any children who have not been given a label beyond the general one of having special educational needs (SEN)?

Changing terminology

In the 1970s, when a committee chaired by Mary Warnock was asked to look into the education of children and young people who, at that time, were described as **handicapped**, the emphasis was on placing pupils in categories of handicap, rather than seeing them first and foremost as unique individuals. The small percentage of pupils who were seen as being handicapped were likely to be educated in a special school catering for that particular type of need. Little account was taken of whether or not their difficulty meant that they had the cognitive ability to benefit from being in a mainstream classroom. There are people today, many of them with a physical disability, who feel resentful that they were not allowed to attend their local schools.

Although the term SEN was introduced to encourage a move away from focusing on categories of need, to seeing the child first and foremost as an individual, labels have never gone away. Some have been changed to sound less derogatory, such as *learning difficulties*, instead of **educationally subnormal**, or *behavioural, emotional and social difficulties* (BESD), rather than **maladjusted**.

Some of these changes were reflected in the first *SEN Code of Practice* (1994). By the time it was revised in 2001, ASD had become recognised, and dyspraxia had joined dyslexia as another type of specific learning difficulty (SpLD). Since then, dyscalculia and dysgraphia have been recognised under SpLD; ADHD has risen to become the largest group within BESD; and multisensory impairment (MSI) has been added to the other types of sensory needs. Several terms are now used to describe difficulties with spoken language, including *speech, language and communication needs* (SLCN) as a broad description and *specific language impairment* (SLI) to describe a smaller group of those with more significant needs. Figure 1.1 summarises how these labels have altered over time.

SEN and disability

To reflect the 2001 Special Educational Needs and Disability Act (SENDA), which brought together the needs of pupils with SEN and those with a disability, the phrase *SEN and disability* is often used rather than SEN on its own. While *SEN* is an educational term, which seeks to throw light on the educational provision that may be needed, *disability* is a medical term, which does not necessarily encompass any educational implications. There is a significant overlap between these terms, although, as the definition of disability has widened, there is also a group of pupils who are considered disabled who do not have SEN. Figure 1.2 is an attempt to clarify the boundaries between SEN and disability, although it is important to note that this is not a comprehensive mapping of all the conditions, but is designed to give an indication of the overlap between the two terms. Nor is the figure drawn to scale.

In this book, the term 'SEN,' rather than 'SEN and disability' is used, as the book does not directly include those who are disabled but who do not have SEN.

1970s	1994	2001	Current terms
Educationally subnormal	Learning difficulties	Cognition and learning: MLD, SLD, PMLD	Global or general learning difficulties: MLD, SLD, PMLD
	Specific learning difficulties: dyslexia	Cognition and learning; specific learning difficulties: dyslexia and dyspraxia	Specific learning difficulties: dyslexia, dyspraxia, dyscalculia, dysgraphia
Maladjusted	Emotional and behavioural difficulties (EBD)	Behavioural, emotional and social difficulties (BESD)	BESD, including ADHD
Blind	Sensory impairment: visual difficulties	Sensory and/or physical needs: visual difficulties	Visual impairment (VI)
Partially sighted	As above	As above	As above
Deaf	Sensory impairment: hearing difficulties	Sensory and/or physical needs: hearing difficulties	Hearing impairment (HI)
Partially deaf	As above	As above	As above
Physically handicapped	Physical disabilities	Sensory and/or physical needs: physical impairments	Physical impairment or disability (PI/PD) Multisensory impairment (MSI)
Speech defects	Speech and language difficulties	Communication and interaction: speech and language delay/disorder Autism	Specific language impairment (SLI); speech, language and communication needs (SLCN); autistic spectrum disorders (ASD)

Figure 1.1   Changing terms in SEN between the 1970s and the present

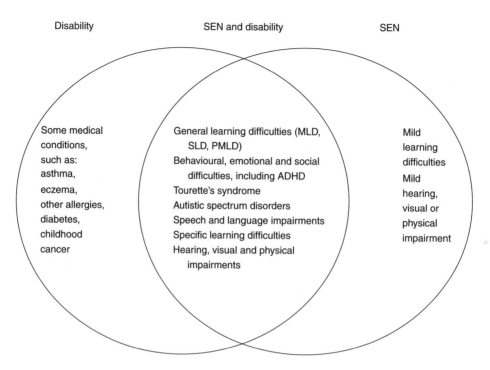

Disability   SEN and disability   SEN

Some medical   General learning difficulties (MLD,   Mild
conditions,   SLD, PMLD)   learning
such as: Behavioural, emotional and social   difficulties
asthma,   difficulties, including ADHD   Mild
eczema,   Tourette's syndrome   hearing,
other allergies,   Autistic spectrum disorders   visual or
diabetes,   Speech and language impairments   physical
childhood   Specific learning difficulties   impairment
cancer   Hearing, visual and physical
                          impairments

Figure 1.2   An indication of the overlap between SEN and disability

Note: This diagram is not comprehensive, nor is it drawn to scale.

>ᘁᘁ Questions for reflection

1   Do you think that most of the labels used today are an improvement on the
    ones used previously?

2   As diagnosis becomes a more refined tool, additional terms are appearing.
    Is this a useful development or not?

3   Do you think it would be more helpful to use the phrase 'SEN and disability,'
    or to clarify the distinction between SEN and disability?

Defining developmental disorders

In general, the term *developmental disorders* is used to describe disorders that are
present in childhood and are thought to have a biological basis. Although many of
the biological markers have not been found, it is thought likely that in some cases
a genetic programming fault of some kind impacts on the normal development of
the brain before birth. In other cases, something else goes wrong in neuronal development during the delicate process of the brain being formed. In either case, this
predisposes children to certain disorders while not actually causing them. These
disorders are sometimes grouped into:

• those where the gene has been identified (for example, Down's syndrome)

• those that are the result of environmental factors (such as Foetal Alcohol Syndrome)

- those of unknown origin

- those where there are neurological abnormalities, the precise nature of which has yet to be determined.

This book does not set out to cover every type of need, or even every type of developmental disorder, but concentrates on this last group. Sometimes, they are referred to as **neurodevelopmental disorders** because it is known that abnormalities in the development of the brain are involved in producing these conditions, even though the actual genes have yet to be identified. The particular group of disorders that are the focus of this book have been selected because they have the following features in common:

1 a biological basis that is not yet fully understood

2 symptoms that overlap with other disorders in this group

3 a tendency to co-exist with each other or with other disorders

4 the disorders appear to be on the increase

5 the disorders are sufficiently prevalent to be of interest to teachers, other professionals and to parents.

Taking these criteria, the book focuses on:

- ADHD

- ASD, including Asperger's syndrome

- specific language impairments (SLI)

- specific learning difficulties (SpLD), including:

  o dyslexia

  o dyspraxia

  o dyscalculia

  o dysgraphia.

Diagnosing developmental disorders

Diagnosing the developmental disorders under consideration in this book is not an exact science. Even ADHD and ASD, which carry a medical diagnosis, will not have the outward signs of a physical illness, so decisions about whether or not to give a child a particular label may not be straightforward. In the main, a diagnosis of a developmental disorder will be made after taking a case history of the child's development, listening to the views of the family and the school, analysing the behaviours the child exhibits and using any relevant assessments.

There are two internationally known reference books that give guidelines for diagnosing the developmental disorders under discussion. These are:

1 *ICD-10*, which is the 10th edition of the *World Health Organisation's International Classification of Diseases*.

2 *DSM-IV-TR*, which is the latest edition of the *American Psychiatric Association's Diagnostic and Statistical Manual of Mental Disorders*.

Apart from the criteria given in *ICD-10* and *DSM-IV-TR*, the training of the professionals undertaking the diagnosis will determine the criteria and assessments they use.

Since the Children Act of 2004, with its emphasis on interagency working, and the development of the Common Assessment Framework (CAF), it is to be hoped that children with difficulties will be picked up at an earlier stage and that any agencies involved will at least be aware of the other professionals working with the child and his or her family. In time, this should help to prevent some children's difficulties becoming entrenched. However, many of the children with the neurodevelopmental disorders, being considered here, will have significant and long-term difficulties that will require a more specialist diagnosis to be made.

As well as the difficulties in making an accurate diagnosis being exacerbated by conditions having overlapping symptoms and sometimes co-existing, another problem can be the child who clearly has difficulties, but who does not present as having enough symptoms under any one heading to merit being given a label at all. These children, along with those who are only mildly affected by a particular condition, are among those where a diagnosis may not be clear-cut. It is comparatively easy to spot the child who has classic autism, severe dyslexia, or a very significant speech and language impairment, but it is much harder to spot these same difficulties in a less extreme form. At the milder end of any continuum or spectrum, there will be a gradual reduction in severity until a condition blends into the normal range. For instance, at what point does the very lively, seemingly wilful child become a candidate for ADHD, or the child who is clumsy and uncoordinated need to be labelled dyspraxic? (All these points about diagnostic labels are discussed in Chapter 3).

⚷ Questions for reflection

1 Are you familiar with the Common Assessment Framework (CAF) and, if so, what do you see as its strengths and limitations?

2 Are there staff at your school who are able to assess some of the kinds of needs under discussion?

3 What links does your school have with other professionals so that pupils can be assessed by someone with the relevant knowledge and training?

4 Are you aware of children who seem to have SEN but who do not fit a particular type of need?

Different disorders

The next part of this chapter discusses the nature of each of the neurodevelopmental disorders that are the focus of this book. Each one is discussed separately, before examining in later chapters, how far they appear to overlap and/or co-occur, and what effect this has on the child's capacity to learn.

The four main disorders are listed in alphabetical order. After each description, there is a photocopiable list of some of the symptoms that may be present. These are not designed to enable the reader to make a diagnosis, but can be used as an indication of whether or not there may be cause for concern. The charts can also be used to give a baseline of a child's performance and to measure the effectiveness of any interventions that take place, by dating the additional columns and recording progress. The charts can be used with individuals whether or not they have a particular label.

Attention deficit hyperactivity disorder (ADHD)

Although there is still some controversy about this diagnosis, there is a growing acceptance of ADHD as a developmental disorder. These are not children who are wilfully naughty, but who have extreme difficulty in controlling their behaviour. The three key symptoms are:

1 inattention

2 impulsiveness

3 hyperactivity.

Originally, children were diagnosed as ADD (attention deficit disorder) or ADHD (attention deficit hyperactivity disorder). Today, it is more usual to talk about three sub-types:

1 predominantly inattentive (as in ADD)

2 predominantly impulsive and hyperactive

3 inattentive, impulsive and hyperactive (combined type ADHD).

ADHD is the most common behavioural disorder. It has been said to affect around 5 per cent of children of school age, with 1 per cent being severely affected. There is a ratio of 4:1 boys to girls, but 1:1 in the inattentive type. Although the next chapter goes into more detail about which conditions co-exist, it is important to mention here that ADHD is more likely to exist alongside other disorders, including **oppositional defiant disorder** (ODD) and **conduct disorder** (CD), than to be present on its own. In his book *Can't Learn, Won't Learn, Don't Care: Troubleshooting Challenging Behaviour*, O'Regan (2006) uses the term 'can't learn' for those with ADHD, 'won't learn' for those with ODD and 'don't care whether they learn or not' for pupils with CD.

Key points ODD and CD

Oppositional defiant disorder (ODD)

Those who have ODD are likely to be negative, defiant and spiteful, arguing with adults and defying rules. They may lose their temper easily, annoy others and blame someone else when things go wrong. Despite constantly upsetting others, they are easily upset themselves.

Conduct disorder (CD)

Those with CD have repetitive and persistent patterns of anti-social behaviour. They are aggressive to people and animals and can be physically cruel. They may bully, start fights and use weapons. They can be deceitful, breaking into cars and houses, and shoplifting or lying to obtain goods. They may be arsonists.

There are two other conditions that are mentioned, both in relation to ADHD and ASD. These are **Gilles de la Tourette's syndrome** (which is commonly abbreviated to 'Tourette's'), sometimes described as the extreme end of ADHD, and **obsessive–compulsive disorder** (OCD). Those with OCD can have obsessions, or compulsions, or both obsessions and compulsions.

Key points Tourette's and OCD

Tourette's syndrome (Gilles de la Tourette's syndrome)

The symptoms include both vocal and motor tics:

- vocal tics – noises (grunts, barks, yelps, etc.), or words (repetition, swearing, etc.)

- motor tics – such as twisting the body, blinking, touching, squatting, or retracing steps when walking.

While others may have tics, those with Tourette's syndrome will have both vocal and motor tics.

Obsessive–compulsive disorder (OCD)

Obsessions are recurrent or persistent thoughts, impulses, or images that cause anxiety or distress, such as tidying up incessantly or rearranging objects.

Compulsions are repetitive behaviours (washing hands, checking), or mental acts (counting, repeating words), which the person feels driven to perform according to rigidly applied rules, as they fear something terrible will happen if the compulsions are not carried out.

Both obsessions and compulsions cause distress, are time consuming and interfere with normal living.

Figure 1.3   Attention deficit hyperactivity disorder (ADHD)

Symptoms	Date	Date	Date	Date	Date	Date
Inattentive/distractable						
Sometimes appears to be in a world of his/her own						
Poor listener; does not always respond when addressed and forgets instructions						
Lacks concentration; flits from one activity to the next; easily bored						
Does not complete tasks; gives up easily and is disorganised and forgetful						
Work is full of errors and untidy						
Distracted by what others are doing, or other events occurring in the vicinity						
Impulsive						
Acts without thinking of consequences; does not plan what to do next						
Calls out and interrupts; does not wait his/her turn; needs instant gratification						
Blurts out answers to questions without thinking						
Talks incessantly; constantly asks questions, but does not wait for answers						
Hyperactive						
Fidgets, fiddles and has boundless energy; always out of his/her seat						
Does not settle to tasks; easily distracted						
Tears about knocking into objects and people; engages in risky physical exploits						

Photocopiable:

Educating Children with Complex Conditions © Winand H. Dittrich and Rona Tutt, 2008.

Autistic spectrum disorders (ASD), including Asperger's syndrome

Autism is a medical diagnosis, which is often given when the child is around three years of age, although people with Asperger's syndrome, may be identified at a much later stage. Today, the term *autistic spectrum disorders* is preferred to autism, as it reflects more closely the fact that autism has many forms. In both *ICD-10* and *DSM-IV-TR*, the term **pervasive developmental disorders** (PDD) is used to cover ASD as well two much rarer conditions: **Rett's syndrome** (which mainly affects girls) and **childhood disintegrative disorder** (CDD). The term PPD-NOS is also used. This stands for a *pervasive developmental disorder – not otherwise specified*. More common in this country is the use of the term *atypical autism* to describe a child who displays some of the symptoms of ASD, but not sufficient for a full diagnosis to be made. The autistic spectrum is often seen as including:

- Kanner's or classic autism

- high-functioning autism

- Asperger's syndrome.

Children with classic autism are likely to have **moderate** to **severe learning difficulties** (MLD or SLD) in addition to their autism. Children with Asperger's syndrome are less entrenched in their own world and may be keen to communicate and to make friends, but their egocentric view of the world and their lack of empathy can cause problems. Although they might be seen as being nearer the norm, life can be hard for them, because they are more aware that they are different, and there is a danger that as they grow older, they may become depressed. Not everyone differentiates between high-functioning autism and Asperger's syndrome, although there may be a valid distinction to be made.

⚷ Key point *The autistic spectrum*

Classic autism	High-functioning autism	Asperger's syndrome
Usually combined with SLD or MLD	*Average or above intelligence*	
The hardest to reach and teach.	Able intellectually but day-to-day living is impaired by the degree of autism.	Less obviously autistic, but still displaying all major aspects of autism. More capable of independent living.

In addition to the triad of impairments (in the areas of communication, socialisation and imagination), children with ASD find it hard to cope with change or to adapt to different social settings. They are often **hyposensitive** (lacking in sensitivity), or **hypersensitive** to: loud noises, too much visual stimulation, the texture of certain clothes, strong smells such as scent, or the taste of all but a very narrow range of foods. They generally find it easier to take in information that is presented visually and they may think in pictures rather than words. Temple Grandin, one of the best known adults with autism, and a world authority on the design of 'humane' slaughterhouses, has described pictures as her first language and words as her second.

The incidence of ASD has risen dramatically, so that it has changed over a comparatively few years from being termed a low incidence need, to one where a figure of 1 in 100 is being suggested. Far more boys than girls are affected. Other conditions may co-occur, but these may be in danger of being overlooked once a diagnosis of ASD is made.

Specific language impairments (SLI)

According to Noam Chomsky, whose ideas on the subject have been largely accepted, humans are pre-programmed to develop language. There are over 6,000 languages in existence, which, between them have 800 different sounds. While acquiring language is an innate ability, learning a particular language will rely on hearing it spoken (or seeing it signed). By the time they are six, children will have mastered most of the sounds of their language (**phonology**), learnt how to produce correct sentences (grammar), fathomed out the meaning that is produced when words are strung together (**semantics**), and become familiar with how to use language (**pragmatics**).

These different areas illustrate the complexity of the young child's task, so perhaps it is not surprising that something can go wrong with any of the aspects of learning to understand what others say (receptive language), or to produce coherent speech (expressive language). The term *specific language impairment* (SLI) is generally used to discuss the group of children whose language development is disordered and not simply delayed. Sometimes the terms *speech*, *language* and *communication* are used almost interchangeably, but there are significant differences between them.

 Key points Speech, language and communication

Speech is a part of language.

Language is a part of communication.

Communication involves spoken and written language, as well as facial expression, posture, gestures and signs.

Children's difficulties with oral language are described in different ways, but they include:

- **phonological disorder** which will result in not being able to reproduce the 44 sounds of the English language

- difficulty with grammar, which may affect how individual words are constructed (**morphology**), or how words are put together in sentences (**syntax**)

- problems with the meaning and the use of language, which is described as a **semantic-pragmatic disorder**.

Figure 1.4 Autistic spectrum disorder (ASD), including Asperger's syndrome

Symptoms	Date	Date	Date	Date	Date	Date
Communication Does not talk or talks very little Does not respond to questions Echolalic (repeating what has been said) May recite chunks of Disney films						
Asperger's syndrome Talks fluently on subjects of interest Poor conversational skills Does not understand non-literal language May have a pedantic manner and unusual intonation						
Social interaction Appears to be in his/her own world Does not seek out physical contact Prefers solitary activities Does not understand about sharing						
Asperger's syndrome Wants to socialise but does not know how Does not pick up on non-verbal cues as to how people are feeling Lacks empathy Gets into arguments and fights						
Imagination Does not play imaginatively Does not indulge in symbolic play Lines objects up rather than playing with them Wants to do the same non-productive activity over and over again						
Asperger's syndrome Good at learning facts and figures; less good at abstract thought Absorbed by narrow range of interests						

Photocopiable:

Educating Children with Complex Conditions © Winand H. Dittrich and Rona Tutt, 2008.

If it is the case, as some suggest, that there are children with semantic-pragmatic difficulties who are not autistic (semantic-pragmatic difficulties being one of the features of the communication impairment of those with ASD), it may be that, like those with atypical autism, they inhabit a grey area between the end of the autistic spectrum and the rest of the population:

Atypical autism		
Autistic spectrum disorders	PDD-NOS	Majority of population
	Semantic-pragmatic disorder	

Other difficulties include:

- *lexical retrieval deficit*, more commonly referred to as *word-finding problems*, where a child struggles to retrieve a word and will use non-specific words and circumlocution instead

- *verbal dyspraxia*, where there is a lack of control over the muscles involved in speech production. (Verbal dyspraxia is also mentioned under specific learning difficulties.)

Other problems, such as **selective/elective mutism**, stammering or stuttering, are not considered in this context, as they may have more of a psychological than a neurological basis. The prevalence of SLI has been given as more than 5 per cent and, once again, more boys than girls have problems in this area. In Figure 1.5, it is important to realise that SLI can take many forms and a child may have combinations of difficulties that go across the headings that have been given.

Specific learning difficulties (SpLD)

Children who have *global* or *general learning difficulties* will be delayed in all areas of their development. These pupils are described as having moderate learning difficulties (MLD), severe learning difficulties (SLD) or **profound and multiple learning difficulties** (PMLD). Pupils with *specific learning difficulties* (SpLD) will have problems not related to their intellectual level, but arising from a neurological abnormality or dysfunction. Although it is easier to detect a specific learning difficulty in children who are within the average or above range of ability, it is possible for children to have both global and specific learning difficulties. In this case, however, it is less likely that any SpLD will be recognised. The four types of SpLD are discussed in the order in which they have become recognised, starting with dyslexia. Children with all types of SpLD have difficulties with organisation, planning and sequencing.

Dyslexia

Children who are dyslexic have difficulty learning to read and to spell. As reading is not a natural activity in the same way as learning to speak, some children will take more time than others to 'crack the code'. It is unfortunate that, unlike languages such as Finnish, German or Italian (which have a one-to-one phoneme–grapheme relationship), English is a very irregular language, which makes it much harder for children to learn the various ways of matching 44 different sounds to the 26 letters of the alphabet.

Figure 1.5 Specific language impairment (SLI)

Symptoms	Date	Date	Date	Date	Date	Date
Phonological/auditory difficulties						
Unable to pronounce all sounds						
Substitutes sounds						
Unable to differentiate between certain sounds						
Unable to separate out the sounds in words						
Gramatical difficulties						
Inclined to give one word replies						
Has difficulty with tenses and plurals						
Has difficulty with conjunctions and prepositions						
Finds it hard to comprehend or use complex sentences						
Semantic difficulties						
Finds it difficult to retain new vocabulary						
Has difficulty understanding new concepts						
May not understand non-literal language						
Has difficulty in expressing his/her thoughts						
Pragmatic difficulties						
Has difficulty in understanding how to adapt language to different social situations						
Makes inappropriate comments						
Semantic-pragmatic disorder						
Has difficulty with both the meaning of words and using language appropriately						
Word-finding difficulties						
Slow to recall words						
Uses non-specific words						
Uses circumlocution						
(Verbal dyspraxia – see Figure 1.6 under 'dyspraxia')						

 Photocopiable:

Much has been made recently of similarities between SLI and dyslexia, with both being seen as having a phonological impairment as a core deficit. However, Bishop and Snowling (2004), who are renowned in the fields of SLI and dyslexia respectively, suggest they should not be seen either as being one condition or as part of the same continuum, but as two separate conditions, albeit with overlapping features.

Dyspraxia/developmental coordination disorder (DCD)

Dyspraxia, or **developmental coordination disorder**, is the term used to describe children who have difficulty coordinating their muscles and therefore both their gross and fine motor development is often affected. At one time, they might have been referred to as 'clumsy', as their lack of spatial awareness and weakness in controlling their movements means they may knock into people and objects or stand abnormally close to them. They have difficulty with orientation and will forget which is left and which is right, or become confused finding their way from place to place. They find it hard to control and judge the accuracy of their movements in terms of direction and speed, particularly when they need to control both at the same time. Their sense of timing is poor, as is their ability to tell the time.

If the muscles used in the production of speech sounds are affected, the children will have verbal dyspraxia as well. Their speech will sound laborious and over-emphatic, as if it is an effort to produce the sounds.

Dyscalculia

This is a term used to describe pupils who have significant difficulty in acquiring mathematical skills, despite making progress in other areas of the curriculum and receiving good teaching. These pupils will have difficulty in understanding and using numbers, or carrying out any calculations involving numbers. They will be prone to sequencing numbers in the wrong order and be unsure which columns to place numbers in when writing out their sums. They will continue to rely on their fingers or other practical apparatus when their peers have moved on to mental calculations. Telling the time and understanding money will also be problematic.

Until recently, very little attention was paid to pupils who struggle with maths, whereas dyslexia has been recognised for many years. As mentioned previously, it is generally accepted that the human brain is pre-programmed to acquire language. In the same way, it is now being suggested that the brain may be hard-wired to handle numbers and to use calculation. Dyscalculia means that, due to a neurological abnormality, the person lacks this innate number sense.

Dysgraphia

Dysgraphia means difficulty in producing handwriting that is legible and which is produced at an age-appropriate speed. It can also include difficulties with content, stemming both from spelling problems and organising thoughts in a way that means they will be coherent on paper. Pupils with dysgraphia may have unusual body posture: leaning to one side, lying across the desk, or altering their posture as the writing moves across the page. They may try to get away with writing as little as possible, or they may show that they can produce more if it is done on the computer. The physical difficulties associated with dysgraphia may be linked to dyspraxia and a lack of control over the muscles.

Figure 1.6 Specific learning difficulties: dyslexia, dyspraxia, dyscalculia, dysgraphia

Symptoms	Date	Date	Date	Date	Date	Date
Dyslexia						
Slow to learn sounds						
Muddles vowel sounds						
Slow to blend words						
Sequences letters incorrectly						
Copies down incorrectly						
Disorganised						
Needs time to process spoken language						
Weak speller						
Dyspraxia						
Bumps into objects and people						
Runs with awkward gait						
Slow to learn to hop and skip						
Finds it difficult to balance, stand on one leg or kick a ball						
Slow to learn correct pencil grip						
Slow to dress and undress						
Verbal dyspraxia						
Exaggerated movements of mouth						
Makes undue effort to pronounce words						
Words not clear, but sounds as if talking when mouth is full						
Dyscalculia						
Lacks intuitive number sense						
Difficulty in sequencing numbers and counting						
Very slow to pick up number concepts						
When writing out sums, puts numbers in wrong columns						
Difficulty with direction, shape and space						
Slow to understand money or tell the time						
Dysgraphia						
Letters poorly formed						
Handwriting untidy						
Often writes very little						
Difficulty organising ideas to put them on to paper						
Body posture abnormal: lying on desk or moving across desk as writing moves across page						

Photocopiable:

Educating Children with Complex Conditions © Winand H. Dittrich and Rona Tutt, 2008.

It is reckoned that up to 10 per cent may be affected to some extent by dyslexia, with more boys than girls having the disorder. Not so much is known about the prevalence of other types of SpLD. It is interesting to note that not only may children have more than one type of specific learning difficulty (so that there is **co-morbidity** between them), but there are seen to be close links between specific learning difficulties and the other conditions being considered. These links are investigated further in subsequent chapters.

In this chapter, a group of four neurodevelopmental disorders has been the focus of the discussion, and the notion has been introduced that there is a degree of overlap and co-morbidity between them. This is explored further in the next chapter, in the context of what has been discovered about the underlying causes of these conditions.

Summary

Despite attempts to reduce the number of labels children are given and to focus instead on their needs, more children are being labelled.

Partly as a result of this, it is becoming increasingly common for children to be given more than one label. This raises the question of how far disorders overlap and/or co-exist.

There would appear to be a group of neurodevelopmental disorders, which seem very different, yet closer examination shows that they have much in common.

The following chapters will consider the neurological abnormalities of these disorders, how they affect children's learning, and how all pupils can be helped to become successful learners.

Further Reading

Chiat, S. (2000) *Understanding Children with Language Problems.* Cambridge: Cambridge University Press.

Hannell, G. (2006) *Identifying Children with Special Needs.* Thousand Oaks, CA: Corwin Press.

Jackson, J. (2004) *Multicoloured Mayhem.* London: Jessica Kingsley.

O'Regan, F. (2006) *Can't Learn, Won't Learn, Don't Care: Troubleshooting Challenging Behaviour.* London: Continuum.

2

The brain, developmental disorders and their effects on learning

This chapter covers:

- the nature of learning and the part that memory plays in the learning process
- how the brain develops and learns
- the **aetiology** of developmental disorders and how far they share the same neurological abnormalities
- what is known about the causes of neurodevelopmental disorders and their co-morbidity
- how particular difficulties are likely to impede a child's ability to learn.

The nature of learning

Learning is the process by which we acquire knowledge and skills. What can be learned, how much and how fast depends on the working of the brain. In the last few years, educators and brain scientists have become increasingly aware of the need to work together, but so far, there is very little in the way of reliable results encompassing the work of these different disciplines. Yet it is clear that neuroscience can illuminate the nature of learning. Studying the brain will help to unravel the mysteries about learning and distinguish between:

- what is well known, like the brain's plasticity or its ability to change

- what may be the case, such as critical periods for learning

- what is intelligent speculation, like the implications for gender

- what are gross oversimplifications, such as the role of the left/right halves of the brain.

The ability to learn can be increased if those who are involved in education understand what is involved in the learning process, as the brain can be partly shaped through teaching and learning. While children's potential will vary according to their genetic inheritance, the effect of the environment plays a crucial role. For instance, for the sensory areas of the brain to develop properly, a child's environment will need to contain a variety of **visual**, **auditory** and **tactile stimuli**. Even before birth, the foetus can hear through the womb in the latter stages of pregnancy and the olfactory sense develops as well, so that newborn babies have little difficulty in recognising their mother by her voice or by her smell. For pupils whose potential may be more limited by their special educational needs (SEN), it is especially important for teaching to be delivered in ways that facilitate and enhance the child's ability to learn.

The brain improves with exercise just like any other organ or muscle. Learning does not necessarily increase the number of brain cells, but it does increase their thickness, their branching and wiring to form complex networks. When experiences are repeated involving the same brain cells, the ability to learn is strengthened. 'Use it or lose it' may apply as much to the mental activity of using the brain as to physical activity. Learning involves not only the acquisition of new knowledge and skills, but being able to retain what has been learned, so that it can be used in the future. Memory is the process by which this is achieved.

 Key points Learning and Memory

The brain is the stage on which all learning and memory occurs.

Learning depends on experience and refers to the acquisition of knowledge and skills. It is the platform for changing behaviour.

Memory is the process by which we store, activate and retain knowledge and skills, to be recalled and put to use at a later date.

Once a baby is born he or she starts to learn by becoming familiar with the structure and routines of the environment and the events that occur regularly within it, such as waking and sleeping, being bathed, changed and fed. Infants' interest in an event is aroused when the unexpected happens and the routine varies in some way. The discrepancy principle (when learning takes place through the unexpected) has implications that can be implemented in the classroom. In their earliest months, babies also learn by *reproducing* or *repeating* human behaviour. By their second birthday, infants are motivated to engage in learning by *imitation*, because they want to behave like other people they have observed.

Between the ages of three and four, children begin to *problem solve*, using their learning and knowledge to work out what to do in a similar situation to one that has arisen before. Next, they are ready to learn in a more conscious way, both through formal teaching and through their own insight into a task (self-teaching). Their desire to understand the relationship between events and explain the physical and social structure in their environment, means that they start to link *cause and effect*, which engages them in thinking and reasoning. This allows them to make predictions and to act upon all kinds of expectations, both real and imaginary.

Every learning experience leads to changes in the brain. However, only changes that are cumulative, repeatedly activated, or fit into **sensitive periods** for learning, will ensure that learning becomes permanent, through the formation of a memory trace in the brain. There are two main types of memory: *the working memory* and the *long-term memory*.

 Key points Different types of memory

The *working memory* has three components:

1   a central executive that controls the two short-term stores, as well as linking with other cognitive systems including long-term memory

2   a short-term store of verbal input

3   a short-term store of visual and spatial input.

The *long-term memory* can be split into:

- an **autobiographical memory** for remembering significant personal events

- a **procedural memory** for storing skills that have been mastered and can be used automatically (such as swimming or driving a car)

- a **declarative memory** divided into:

    1   **episodic memory** for storing incidents in the recent past

    2   **semantic memory** for storing facts, word meanings and general knowledge.

The working memory is able to retain or distribute information, either verbally or visually, while also engaged in attention. The brain's frontal lobes are strongly involved. Teaching that concentrates mainly on delivering facts and abstract information may soon overstretch pupils' working memory. The long-term memory enables information to be transferred to long-term storage networks.

How the brain develops

Initially, the developing brain has a smooth surface. Later, the brain divides first into two halves and then into the separate lobes. All **neurons** (brain cells) are generated in one small area deep inside the brain known as the **germination area**. Once generated, the neurons have to find their way to specific locations.

This process is called **neuronal migration**. It happens in waves and brain layers are formed accordingly, starting with the deepest layers and finishing with the ones nearest to the surface. After finishing the migration, neurons start forming connections to neighbouring neurons to create interactive networks. The organisation, structure and complexity of brain development is extraordinary, and that is why some scientists claim that the brain is the most amazing and beautiful structure in the world.

All through this period in the womb, environmental conditions can affect prenatal development and the precise nature of that effect will depend on the stage of development that has been reached. This is the time when the nervous system, the internal organs, the limbs, and various structures, such as the eyes and ears, are being formed.

In the first few months after birth, there is rapid development in the sensory and motor areas of the brain. This seems to correspond with a time when there is rapid development of the child's perceptual abilities. From animal studies, it is clear that there are strong links between the child's sensory and motor experiences and actual brain growth. For example, kittens that are raised in an environment where there are no vertical lines but only horizontal ones, lose the ability to perceive horizontal lines accurately. Animals living in such an environment have fewer brain cells that respond to that kind of visual input. This shows that the interaction of sensory information with movements or actions appears to be crucial, not only for cell survival, but for cognitive development as well. Although Piaget's view of the stages of children's development has been superseded by infants being seen as thinkers and problem solvers, he was right to emphasis the importance of interaction in the development of **sensorimotor coordination**.

Quite likely, the brain is 'pre-wired' for certain sensory and motor functions (for example, perceiving depth and faces, and coordinating eye–hand movements), but that this pre-wiring has to be used in order for it to continue to function. Sensitive periods for learning are times when, if the environmental stimulation is present, the brain's sensory and motor systems will develop normally. These periods may not be rigid and inflexible, but may be temporary windows that help the development of the brain at particular times, provided the environment is adequate. Nature and nurture need to combine for a child to develop normally.

Neurons represent the functioning core of the brain and of the whole nervous system. Each neuron has tens of thousands of branch-like structures called **dendrites**, which emerge from the neurons and transmit the electrical impulses they receive along fibres called **axons**. (Each neuron has one axon). Axons are surrounded by a layer known as the **myelin sheath**. Between each dendrite of one cell and the axon of the next cell is a tiny gap called the **synapse**. The neuron sends electrical impulses through the axon to the synapse, where the activity releases chemicals, which start another neuron's activities. These chemicals are known as **neurotransmitters**, the most common of which are **adrenaline, serotonin** and **dopamine**. Learning occurs when the synapses create physical and chemical changes. Repeated 'firings' enhance the formation of a memory. By the electrical and chemical stimulation of the cells, information is spread and stored all over the brain. A second type of cells known as **glial** (or support) cells hold the neurons together, keeping out substances that are harmful to neurons.

In the fifth month after conception half the cells die off, ensuring that only the neurons that have made connections survive. By the time babies are born, they have most of the brain cells they need. After birth, the number of connections between the brain cells increases very rapidly, to the extent that it far exceeds those of the adult brain. Nerve fibres thicken and rewire to enable the full range of brain activities to be undertaken. By puberty, the connections that are useful frequently become permanent, while most of the unused ones have disappeared. The richer the environment, the more connections are made between the cells. Conclusions that can be drawn from brain research into neural development, which are relevant to education, may be summarised as follows:

- Brain connections made during the first year after birth are vital.

- New connections for social behaviours may emerge much later (16–24 years of age).

- Sensitive periods are narrow opportunities for brain development that need to be utilised.

- Enriched environments lead to more cell connections than deprived ones.

- Brain plasticity and **restitution** of function is enormous, if trained or used.

How the brain learns

In traditional forms of teaching, the teacher was there to impart knowledge while the student's role was to receive the information and act on it. Now, it is recognised that learning should be an active experience, which goes beyond absorbing knowledge derived from the materials being offered, to recognising a whole set of conditions under which learning can take place. While they are learning and forming memories, children are engaged in quite complex activities involving the whole behavioural system of the brain.

The brain may be divided into three parts. These are the **forebrain**, the **cerebellum** and the **brainstem**. The forebrain is the uppermost part of the brain, and is composed of the **cerebrum**, (which is 80 per cent of the brain), the **limbic system**, and the **thalamus** and **hypothalamus**. As a general rule, the regions towards the centre and the bottom of the brain are concerned with balancing internal and automatic body functions, and with relaying information to and from the outer parts. Interior parts of the brain that are relevant to the neurological impairments found in the developmental disorders being considered include: the brain stem, which is the oldest and deepest part of the brain, controlling vital functions such as breathing, body temperature, blood pressure and digestion, and the cerebellum (or little brain), which is at the back of the brain, and is involved in learning, and in coordinating movement and balance.

Areas towards the top and outer regions of the brain are involved in perceptual skills, motor learning and abstract cognitive activities. The cerebrum is the upper and largest part of the brain. It includes the cerebral **cortex**, which is the outermost layer. The two halves of the cerebrum are separate apart from being linked by a small bridge-like structure of connecting fibres. The left **hemisphere** controls the right side of the body and is concerned with language. It takes an organised approach, analysing facts, processing information and looking for detail. The right hemisphere controls the left side of the body. It takes a more global approach, pulling together information from different sources in order to draw conclusions. It is also concerned with visual imagination and with emotion.

The brain also has four major exterior lobes (see Figures 2.1 and 2.2) which relate to divisions of the cortex (or outer layer of the brain):

- The **frontal lobe** is the largest and is sometimes referred to as the **executive control** centre, as it monitors higher-order thinking, directs the planning of actions and decision making, instigates problem solving, and regulates the excesses of the emotional system. The frontal lobe continues to mature into early adulthood, so it is not fully operational during adolescence.

- The **temporal lobe** includes areas concerned with learning and memory. It also houses the speech centre of the brain.

- The **occipital lobe** mainly processes visual information.

- The **parietal lobe** is responsible for sensory integration and orientation, linking together perception and spatial awareness.

The **motor cortex** controls the movements of the body and the **somatosensory cortex** processes all the touch signals of the body.

The limbic system consists of several structures that seem to be important in processing emotions, as well as shaping learning and memory. The **amygdala** plays an important part in processing emotion. The **hippocampus** plays a major role in consolidating learning and in converting information from the working memory to the long-term storage regions. The **thalamus** is a pivotal structure in the flow of information in the brain, directing sensory information to appropriate points in the cerebrum. It also relays information going out to the skeletal muscles from the motor cortex or cerebellum. The hypothalamus plays an important part in people's emotions and motivation, and on our reaction to stress, that can either support or hinder learning.

The **basal ganglia** are groups of cells strongly linked to the thalamus and frontal cortex that appears to monitor and adjust all kinds of motor behaviour, as well as having a crucial role in certain cognitive processes, such as learning and attention.

As well as the external sensory input, such as seeing or hearing, there are internal senses that regulate the body's activities: the **tactile sense**, the **vestibular sense** (controlling balance), and the **proprioceptive sense** (coordinating the body's position and movements). Learning difficulties of any kind are instances when the conditions for learning are somehow wrong. This is often the result of a number of factors coming together and disrupting learning.

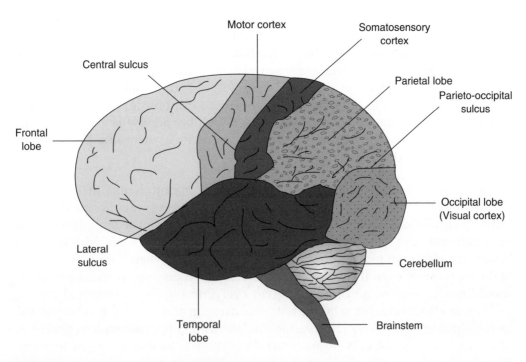

Figure 2.1 Sketch of the brain and its structures

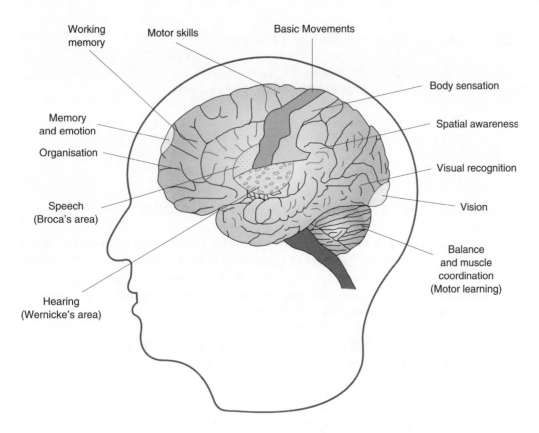

Figure 2.2 Sketch of the brain and some psychological functions
Note: Functions should not be seen as restricted to small areas only but widely distributed normally.

In the medical journal, *The Lancet* (9 Feb 2002), the amazing story of a seven-year-old girl was published. At a very young age she had suffered from life-threatening **meningitis**, and at the age of three her left brain hemisphere had to be removed to prevent uncontrollable **epileptic** fits. As this is the half that controls language, the absence of verbal communication as well as severe movement disability down one side of the body would be expected. Yet this seven-year-old girl had no significant disabilities and spoke two languages fluently. This is an extreme demonstration of how flexible and adaptable the brain is. Compensation and learning are the key words in this example. The remaining half of the brain adapted to its new role and used its established connections in a completely different way.

It may seem to be something of a paradox that a minor change in the brain's physiology while developing in the womb, may have a very significant effect on learning and behaviour, yet, there are cases where up to half the brain is removed in childhood and yet does not have a substantial effect on learning and behaviour. This is an indication of what may be possible when both halves of the brain are present, even if they suffer some damage. It also means failure to learn should not be seen as an option. It gives everyone hope that potential can be used more effectively. For schools, both mainstream and special, it is important to keep in mind that every child can learn. Unleashing the tremendous potential of each individual can only be achieved if the brain is used in the right way and engages in activities that make the best use of its immense capacity.

 Key points Adaptation and the brain

The brain's **plasticity** enables it to adapt to changing circumstances, although this depends to a large extent on how much it is used.

The brain's **resilience** enables it to respond to injury by cells taking over some of the tasks previously performed by those that have been damaged.

Neurological impairments in different disorders

Although it is becoming increasingly clear that the disorders are unlikely to have a single cause, but are likely to result in impairments of different areas of the brain, and/or in the neurological systems that bring together different pieces of information, it needs to be remembered that studies mapping brain areas to neurodevelopmental disorders are still in their infancy.

The next part of this chapter considers the possible causes, as far as they are known, of the four types of disorders outlined in the first chapter.

Attention deficit hyperactivity disorder (ADHD)

ADHD is thought to be caused by multiple genetic and environmental risk factors working together. This means that the disorder runs in families, but that certain environmental conditions make a person more likely to develop ADHD. For instance, although chemicals in the diet, poor parenting or spending too much time on activities such as computer games may exacerbate the condition, they would be unlikely to cause ADHD.

Although no single part of the brain is involved in regulating behaviour, it would appear that the frontal lobes are the main areas involved. To sustain attention, parts of the frontal lobes have to reach a certain level of maturity and it is possible that the frontal lobes develop at a slower rate in ADHD children, making it harder for them to concentrate and to control their behaviour. The **prefrontal cortex** helps planning, decision making, attentional control and the inhibition of inappropriate behaviour. Other features that have been suggested as part of the brain features and functioning of those who have ADHD include: the ADHD brain being 5 per cent smaller than normal and consuming less **glucose** (its main fuel source), especially in the frontal lobe regions, where slower brain waves are also apparent; increased activity or an imbalance in certain neurotransmitters, most likely dopamine and serotonin; differences in the parts of the brain responsible for voluntary movement, including the basal ganglia with their connections to the prefrontal cortex, which send commands about starting and stopping movements; an imbalance between the input of the still immature centres of the right hemisphere/**anterior cingulate** that focuses attention, and the prefrontal area that selects goals and plans how to reach them.

Autistic spectrum disorders (ASD)

Autism is a condition which is believed to be among the most genetically based of the neurodevelopmental disorders, with high heritability. There is general agreement that no single brain abnormality can explain the cause of autism. At the present time, it is thought most likely that ASD, like ADHD, is the result of a genetic predisposition impacting on brain development before birth, which is then triggered by environmental influences. The *impairments* may be the outcome of an underlying brain abnormality and/or problems in a child's early emerging neural system. ASD brains have been shown to differ in their structure.

Studies of brain tissue show that the limbic brain (including the hippocampus and amygdala), is most often abnormal in ASD, with increased packing density, smaller neurons, and reduced blood flow. Limbic damage or abnormalities could be expected to result in the following (all of which are features of ASD): memory impairments, desire for sameness, anxiety, poor **perception** of facial features and emotion, difficulties with social interaction and with language, seizures, sensory deficits, repetitive behaviours.

In addition, the social mechanisms for relating to other people and understanding their intentions and ideas exist in the following areas: *the medial pre-frontal cortex* (monitoring the internal state of self and others), *the superior temporal sulcus* (recognising and analysing people's movements and actions), and the temporal poles adjacent to the amygdala, (processing emotions). These three areas are thought to play a crucial part in *mentalising*, that is to say, understanding how other people think and feel, and being able to empathise with them. These areas may have developed differently compared to other people.

Medical examinations suggest that around 50 per cent of those who have ASD have some evidence of brain stem damage or dysfunction, an imbalance of certain neurotransmitters, in particular a relative increase in dopamine-breakdown products, and the mechanisms to do with the neurotransmitter serotonin, as well as abnormalities in the cerebellum, brain stem and frontal and temporal lobes, in particular the amygdala. These parts of the brain are responsible for aspects that are features of autism:

- The temporal lobes (**Wernicke's area**) are crucial for understanding spoken language. The amygdala coordinates social interaction.

- The brain stem sorts out incoming sensory stimuli.

- The cerebellum coordinates motor movements, including those involved in social interaction.

- The frontal lobes deal with executive functions (planning, motivation, time concepts and impulse control).

Research has moved a long way from Bruno Bettelheim's purely psychogenic model of autism in the 1960s to the present-day focus on the interaction of genes and the environment in the form of brain–behavioural relationships. Despite inconsistent findings about differences in the working of the intact brain in imaging studies, one finding has come up again and again. There is evidence emerging that the brain of people with autism is larger and heavier compared to the rest of the population. It is unclear why this is the case, although it could be that initial cell connections have not been reduced.

Specific language impairment (SLI)

It is thought that at least some forms of specific language impairment have a heritable component and that the nature of the neurological abnormality may vary depending on the type of difficulty the person has with understanding and using language.

The left hemisphere of the brain is where most operations occur that are to do with language, although in left-handed people both sides seem to be equally involved. The processing of grammar and of vocabulary appear to rely on different neural systems within the brain. Grammatical and lexical-retrieval impairments (word-finding problems) are associated with dysfunctions of the basal ganglia, especially the **caudate nucleus**, and of the frontal cortex, particularly **Broca's area** (a region of the left frontal lobe dedicated to the production of speech). Semantic processing (dealing with the meaning of words) appears to occur in the posterior regions of both the right and left hemispheres of the brain, while grammatical processing may use only the left hemisphere.

Although SLI is a language disorder, its linguistic impairments co-occur with non-linguistic deficits, including impairments in motor skills and **working memory**. Children whose SLI takes the form of verbal dyspraxia have already been mentioned in the first chapter. In this case, the link between language impairment and difficulties with movement is clear. But there are others with SLI who have been found to have associated motor impairments, particularly in tasks involving rapid movements or complex sequential motor skills. This offers some support to the notion that individuals with SLI have impairments in sequencing, speed, timing and balance due to deficits of the procedural memory system, which is caused by a dysfunction of the frontal/basal ganglia circuits or the cerebellum. The frontal/basal ganglia circuits, especially the caudate nucleus, play a major role in the procedural memory system, which uses unconscious memory for the production of motor skills. As well as being instrumental in the production of speech and abstract thought, Broca's area is involved with the cognitive aspects of procedural memory, as well as motor functions.

Specific learning difficulties (SpLD)

Although there seems to be an underlying genetic cause of specific learning difficulties, no single neurological abnormality can account for the different, albeit overlapping, symptoms that appear in dyslexia, dyspraxia, dyscalculia and dysgraphia.

Dyslexia

There is clearly a link between speaking and reading, and a secure basis in oral language will lay the foundation for learning to read. However, unlike learning to speak, learning to read is not a natural process, so reading may not have been incorporated into the genetic code as yet. Reading involves the coordination of three processes linked to different neural pathways:

1   Visual processing (**orthography**)

2   Sound recognition (phonology)

3   Word interpretation (semantics).

So the visual and auditory processing systems are involved, as well as the frontal lobe, which will search long-term memory sites for meaning. The translation of letters and sounds is thought to occur in the *angular gyrus*, which lies at the border of the temporal and parietal lobes. The parietal lobe itself has the association of the written word with the spoken word as one of its functions. The temporal lobe contains Wernicke's area, which is involved in decoding language, and the **planum temporale**, which is of importance in mastering the alphabetic code. The area at the back of the left temporal lobe is thought to be the region where whole words are stored and retrieved.

Dyscalculia

As even very young babies seem to have a rudimentary concept of number, it has been suggested that, in the same way that children are pre-programmed to learn language, they may be born with an innate number sense. Although there is considerable overlap and people cannot be divided neatly into the two categories, there may be biological reasons why men are often better at analysing, constructing systems and spatial tasks, while women are better at empathising and verbal tasks. However, this general statement does not allow for the fact that every individual is different and this uniqueness can override the differences between the male and female brain, as demonstrated by the amazing life stories of the **Polgar sisters**.

There would appear to be several areas of the brain that are concerned with mathematical concepts and calculations. However, it is not clear whether dyscalculia is caused by damage to one or more areas, or a failure to integrate information from various sources. Different areas of the **visual cortex** are each responsible for reading digits and reading number words. The parietal cortex (including the basal ganglia, motor and somatosensory cortex) is used for many mathematical calculations, including multiplication, comparison, quantity, and **visuo-spatial processing in memory**. There is a high correlation between mathematical ability and spatial ability. More often than not, people who are good at finding their way around different environments and have a good sense of direction will not have difficulty picking up and understanding mathematical concepts.

Dysgraphia

As the most recent of the four specific learning difficulties to be identified, less is known about the nature and origin of dysgraphia than the other SpLD. However, it is seen as a neurological disorder that may stem from different causes, including deficits in phoneme-to-grapheme conversion, which is an operation of the angular gyrus, deficits in spatial processing systems of the brain's right hemisphere, or deficits in muscle control involving the fingers, wrist and hand. It is important to remember that the brain's motor cortex is not fully developed until the age of five or later, and that boys, on the whole, mature more slowly than girls.

Dyspraxia

There is thought to be a neurological basis for sensorimotor coordination difficulties, with more than one part of the brain being involved. As large areas of the brain assist in maintaining balance and posture, even a small abnormality may result in poor motor control.

The cerebellum plays a leading role in movement. Impairments in the cerebellum can lead to difficulties in coordinating movement, in balancing, and a whole range of activities which rely on gross or fine motor skills: catching and throwing a ball, skipping and hopping, using a pencil, or playing a percussion instrument. The frontal cortex is involved in motor memory, while the basal ganglia and hippocampus store memories of similar movements having been used in the past.

So far, the discussion has been mainly around ADHD, ASD, SLI and SpLD, although conduct disorder (CD), obsessive–compulsive disorder (OCD), oppositional defiant disorder (ODD) and Tourette's syndrome were mentioned in the previous chapter, because they have been found to co-occur with the developmental disorders under discussion. So, it is worth looking at what is known about their aetiology.

Oppositional defiant disorder (ODD) and conduct disorder (CD)

ODD is thought to result from the interplay of three factors: a genetic vulnerability, a biological abnormality, such as an imbalance in certain chemicals in the brain, and an unsatisfactory environment, such as a dysfunctional family life, with violence, inconsistent discipline, unstable relationships and a history of mental illness. CD is sometimes thought of as the more severe form of ODD. As with ODD, the same three elements are likely to be the cause, with the environmental factors including unsatisfactory parenting and an absence of bonding. Indeed, the lack of appropriate role models seems to be a factor in whether or not children develop CD.

Before the frontal cortex is mature enough to act as a start–stop function, adults caring for the infant act as the control, and most infants will respond to these external directions. Children with CD or ODD do not seem able to respond in this way. Once they reach school age, this has an impact on their ability to behave in a way that allows them to respond positively to the learning opportunities that are offered.

Obsessive–compulsive disorder (OCD)

There are different theories about the origin of OCD, with some viewing it as a psychological disorder which can be traced to a traumatic event in childhood; some seeing it following a genetic pattern where one or both parents have obsessional behaviour; while others, perhaps a majority, think its roots lie in abnormalities in the brain. In this case, it is suggested that in OCD, communication between the front part of the brain (the **orbitofrontal cortex**), the caudate nucleus (which lies between the orbitofrontal cortex and the thalamus), and the thalamus is faulty, because of insufficient levels of serotonin, which is the major messenger in this area. This causes the thalamus to become overactive, creating a loop of never-ending worry signals. If children's thoughts are taken up with needless concerns, it becomes difficult for them to concentrate on learning.

Tourette's syndrome

Tourette's is thought to be caused by a genetic vulnerability that results in a neurological impairment of the central nervous system. Although the precise causes have yet to be pinpointed, once again, the brain chemical dopamine, and possibly other brain chemicals, are being implicated. Tics use up some of the nervous energy that would otherwise be available to support learning.

Co-morbidity between developmental disorders

For many co-existing behavioural and mental difficulties there is a strong correlation with developmental differences in relation to the structures and workings of the brain. Understanding children with complex conditions in terms of brain functions still has a long way to go, but enough has been discovered to indicate that this will be a profitable area for further research and new approaches to learning.

At the present time, it would appear that ADHD has such a high rate of co-morbidity, that it is more common for ADHD to appear with other disorders, than for it to exist on its own. It has been suggested that there is a co-morbidity rate of as much as 45 per cent with SLI and possibly 40 per cent with SpLD (although it is not clear which types of SpLD this includes). In addition, it has been said that as many as half the children with ADHD may also have ODD or CD, and that some will have OCD or Tourette's syndrome. ADHD and ASD are increasingly being found to co-exist. ADHD, then, can be seen as a link between all the developmental disorders under discussion, as well as with ODD, CD, OCD and Tourette's syndrome.

Looking at the links from the ASD angle, the closeness of ASD and SLI is apparent in the debate about semantic-pragmatic disorder (which is covered elsewhere in this book). It is not easy to separate out those children with ASD who have additional language impairments as well, so while there may be no clear figures in terms of percentages, it is not uncommon to find children with ASD who also have SLI. Nor is it unusual to find children who have both ASD and a specific learning difficulty. Although a percentage have **hyperlexia**, (where their ability to read fluently outstrips their comprehension), others may have dyslexia, dysgraphia or dyscalculia in addition to their autism. It is interesting to note that while children with classic autism are often well coordinated, those who have Asperger's syndrome tend to be less well coordinated and some are found to have dyspraxia.

There are obvious links between SLI and specific learning difficulties, in that difficulties with aspects of spoken language may lead to difficulty in acquiring literacy skills and the possibility that they have a similar neurological abnormality in common. Both learning to read and learning to speak depend, at least in part, on phonological skills, and there is, in fact, a high co-morbidity rate between SLI and the specific learning difficulty of dyslexia, while the link with dyspraxia (through verbal dyspraxia) has already been referred to.

The overlap and co-existence between SpLD and the other three groups of disorders has already been mentioned. In addition, it is important to bear in mind that specific learning difficulties often co-exist with each other. For instance, while about 4 per cent of the population is said to have dyscalculia (although the figure may be higher, as little has been done until recently to diagnose it), it is not known how many of these also have dyslexia, but there is some evidence of the co-existence of these two types of specific learning difficulties, as there is with others in this group of difficulties. In the case study, Sylvie (see Chapter 1), for example, was a student who had dyslexia and dyspraxia. A recent study of disorders co-existing with dyspraxia found that only 14 per cent had dyspraxia as a single condition (see Chapter 5, page 79).

At the current time, it is not possible to be too definite about which disorders co-exist or how often they may do so. It is by no means unusual for co-morbidity to occur, but, once a diagnosis has been made, other conditions are not always sought or recognised. Even so, there is some evidence that in the case of at least two of the disorders (ADHD and dyspraxia), it is far more common for them to exist with other conditions than to appear on their own.

〰 Questions for reflection

1   Of what practical help do you think it might be to have some understanding of the causes of developmental disorders?

2   How do you reconcile what has been discussed about the way neurological impairments may be partly responsible for the disorders children have, with the case of the girl who had half her brain removed?

3   Looking at the children you know who have been given a diagnosis of one of the disorders being discussed, do you think it makes sense to say that a proportion of them may have co-existing conditions?

Summary

Learning is the process by which we acquire knowledge and learn new skills. Memory enables us to remember information and to store it, so that it can be retrieved later.

Understanding how the brain operates provides an insight into how to support pupils who have difficulties in learning how to learn, or in learning how to behave. This includes those who have developmental disorders.

Neurological impairments that have a genetic/biological basis would appear to be a root cause of the developmental disorders ADHD, ASD, SLI and SpLD. Environmental factors may act as triggers in children who are predisposed to developing certain conditions.

Although it is not possible to say with any certainty how often neurodevelopmental disorders may co-exist with each other or with other conditions, it is becoming apparent that some disorders are more likely to co-exist than to be present on their own.

Further Reading 📖

Blakemore, S.-J. and Frith, U. (2005) *The Learning Brain: Lessons for Education*. Oxford: Blackwell.

Gathercole, S.E. and Alloway, T.P. (2008) *Working Memory and Learning*. London: Sage Publications.

Milne, D. (2005) *Teaching the Brain to Read*. Hungerford: SK Publishing.

Smith, A. (2002) *The Brain's Behind It*. Stafford: Network Educational Press.

3

Fitting labels to children and children to labels

> **This chapter covers:**
>
> - the meaning of labels, different approaches to labelling and who is involved in the process
> - the advantages, disadvantages and complications of labelling, including controversial issues around defining children's needs
> - how the process of labelling is expanding to recognise more disorders
> - the need to keep labelling in perspective, so that meeting the child's needs is seen as paramount.

The meaning of labels

In terms of their education, pupils who have any kind of learning or behavioural difficulties will fall within the general label of having special educational needs (SEN). The majority of pupils with SEN will acquire a further label, which will help to clarify more precisely the nature of their difficulties. Neurodevelopmental disorders are defined by clusters of symptoms and, as more is discovered, the disorders are not being seen as entirely discrete, but as having overlapping symptoms. This can lead to some confusion about:

- which is the right label to give

- whether to give more than one label

- what to do about the child or young person who does not fall clearly within any diagnostic label, yet clearly has difficulties.

Diagnosis relies heavily on observing the child's behaviour, together with hearing accounts by others who know the child, of the behaviours they have observed. This means that much will depend on the skill of diagnosticians, their background, training and experience, particularly if they are working on their own rather than as part of a group of professionals.

A disorder or syndrome may be named after the cluster of symptoms, such as in the case of attention deficit hyperactivity disorder (ADHD), obsessive–compulsive disorder (OCD), or oppositional defiant disorder (ODD), or named after the person who identified it, as in the cases of Kanner's autism, Asperger's syndrome, and Gilles de la Tourette's syndrome.

Approaches to labelling

In the context of SEN, labelling children's behavioural patterns has been guided by a *medical model*. This model is characterised by a performance deficit approach, whereby the focus is on identifying what the child is unable to do. In this model, the limitations a child is seen as having are viewed solely in terms of biological deficits. As well as providing an assessment of the nature of a child's difficulties, the label may be used to indicate the educational provision or support that is felt to be necessary, including any interventions that will help remediate the child's difficulties.

For many years, the medical model has been challenged by a value-based approach known as a *social model*. In contrast to the medical approach, this approach sees the problems being caused by societal attitudes to those who are different. Therefore, it is society itself that needs to make changes rather than the individual. Although the social model has not replaced the medical model, it has helped to raise public awareness of what needs to be done to ensure that those with SEN and disability are included as fully as possible in society.

More recently, approaches have been developed which draw on both the medical and social models. These include a *cognitive neuropsychological model* which accepts the need to investigate neurological causes as well as environmental factors, in order to discover how the brain works. This approach is the most holistic, as it allows for the plasticity of the brain and the child's ability to change to be recognised, as well as broader environmental factors, including the influence of the home, the school and the wider community. Applying this approach to education means that knowledge about the brain–behaviour relationship seems crucial in understanding how to help pupils to learn.

It was, perhaps, unhelpful that the social model swung too far away from the medical model by suggesting that a change in attitude on the part of society, even accompanied by the necessary legislation, was all that was needed. The biological and neurological aspects of SEN and disability cannot be ignored, any more than it is sensible to ignore the changes that society needs to make in its attitude to those with SEN and disability, who should be afforded the same opportunities as the non-disabled, in as far as this can be made possible. In education, a more integrated approach is needed, which takes account of both facts and values.

It could be seen as unfortunate that a more complex population has arrived in schools, both special and mainstream, before sufficient training has been put in place to help staff understand children they may not have come across before. The need for such training was identified in the government's SEN strategy of 2004 (*Removing Barriers to Achievement*), but has been delayed (see Chapter 6, page 87).

Questions for reflection

1 What do you see as the strengths and limitations of the medical model?

2 Do you think the social model applies to all types of disability or particularly to those with a physical disability?

3 What more do you think schools, colleges, universities and local communities could do to make it easier for those with SEN and disability to feel included?

Who labels children?

In considering developmental disorders, a diagnosis may be given when a group of symptoms are clustered together. The age of onset, familial incidence, response to treatment and cause or causes help to define the condition further. In medicine, causal features best define categories of illnesses; in psychiatry, symptoms over time may be a better indicator. Overall, a holistic approach to assessment is needed, which involves not just a consideration of all aspects of development, but environmental influences as well. Occasionally, it may even be the case that altering something in the child's environment, whether at home or at school, is enough to overcome any difficulty.

To increase the chances of making a correct diagnosis and not overlooking whether or not the child has more than one condition, a comprehensive assessment of children with learning and/or behavioural difficulties should include:

- listening to the family's account of the child's development and behaviour

- gathering information from the school

- observing the child's behaviour

- conducting formal and informal tests and assessments of the child's:

  o perceptual and sensory functions

  o motor functions

  o intellectual and cognitive functions

  o attention and memory

  o learning and processing capacity

  o communication and language skills

  o mathematical understanding

  o curricular achievements and levels of attainment.

If a comprehensive assessment does not take place, there is a danger that a less experienced practitioner, particularly one who is working on his or her own, may focus on some features, without seeing that a cluster of features taken together may add up to a particular condition or conditions. Brain scans and other procedures have resulted in greater knowledge about the workings of the brain, but they seldom form part of the diagnosis of developmental disorders.

ADHD and ASD are both medical diagnoses, so a doctor, paediatrician or psychiatrist will be involved, while SLI and SpLD do not have to be diagnosed by a medical practitioner. Regardless of whether or not the diagnosis is a medical one, the type of training and experience professionals have had may incline them towards using certain labels and ignoring others. A speech and language therapist (SaLT), for instance, might diagnose a child as having a semantic-pragmatic disorder, while a paediatrician may see the difficulties the same child is having with understanding and using language as being part of ASD.

For schools, the educational psychologist (EP) is the person they are likely to turn to and he or she may be the one to make the diagnosis, or to advise which other specialists need to be involved. SaLTs may take the lead in diagnosing communication difficulties, including specific language impairments (SLI). For dyspraxia, a physiotherapist (physio) and/or an occupational therapist (OT) may make the decision. Dyscalculia and dysgraphia have been recognised comparatively recently, so getting an accurate diagnosis may be harder. However, some of the organisations like the British Dyslexia Association (BDA) or Dyslexia Action (formerly known as the Dyslexia Institute), have widened their area of expertise to recognise the full range of specific learning difficulties. In addition to EPs and the specialist organisations, there are growing numbers of specialist teachers who are qualified to assess dyslexia and some of the other disorders. (See Useful Addresses at end of this book for details of organisations for particular disorders.)

Although *ICD-10* and *DSM-IV-TR* provide lists of symptoms, they rarely define the symptoms with any precision. Even competent and experienced clinicians may differ sharply over whether a symptom is present, or whether it is present to a sufficiently significant degree. Even if they agree that a symptom should count, they may disagree about the diagnostic label to be given to the symptoms. Bearing all this in mind, it is easy to understand why there are marked differences, not only in labelling the disorders in the first place, but also about the degree to which different disorders are seen as co-existing.

〰️ **Questions for reflection**

1 Which professionals have been involved in the assessment of children and young people you know?

2 Are you aware of anywhere in your area that carries out multi-professional assessments of developmental disorders, and, if so, which ones do they specialise in?

3 What do you think would make assessing developmental disorders a more accurate process?

The advantages and disadvantages of labelling

The whole question of giving children labels has been argued fiercely over many decades. Readers will have their own opinion as to whether or not the advantages outweigh the disadvantages.

Advantages of labelling

Some children, particularly if they are very young or have significant difficulties, will be unaware of the label they have been given. For others, a diagnosis can be a relief. There are many examples of children and adults who were relieved when a label was given and they understood why they were experiencing difficulties. In his book, *Glass Half Empty Glass Half Full*, Chris Mitchell describes his life as being in two halves: the periods before and after he had a diagnosis of Asperger's syndrome. Before the label was given, he says he felt like a failure because he was unable to live up to society's expectations of him. He goes on to say:

> Personally, I would not accept a cure for Asperger's syndrome if one became available, as I consider it to be the most important characteristic of who I am, rather than a label. Most of all, I wouldn't want to go back to my pre-diagnosis days. (2005: 94)

Similarly, those who have received a late diagnosis of dyslexia have spoken of their relief that they no longer had to think of themselves as stupid, because they had a reason for their difficulties.

Parents and carers often feel relieved when their child receives a diagnosis. It can take the pressure off them when they realise it is not their parenting skills that are at fault, rather that throwing a tantrum in a public place at an age when other children have outgrown them is not unusual in a child with ASD. It may also provide them with the opportunity to join a support group for families who have children with similar needs. This can be very helpful in preventing a feeling of isolation when they realise other families are experiencing similar problems.

As far as schools are concerned, receiving the right label can guide the school in tailoring any interventions to the needs of the child, whether it is an extra adult to help the pupil with ADHD remain on task, enlisting the aid of a SaLT in devising strategies to help the child with a word-finding problem, or seeking out specialist teaching for a severe dyslexic. It can also help teachers to group similar pupils together when receiving additional support. Like their parents, some children can be relieved to find that there are others like them, while non-disabled children can learn to be more accepting of others, if they are helped to understand why some children behave differently. Many will go out of their way to be friendly and helpful, if they see a child who is struggling or who is lonely, once they realise why the child finds it hard to fit in.

Although it may sometimes be necessary to exclude from school students who have SEN (particularly if they are not in the right environment), the problems they are causing will be seen in a different light when it is realised that the boy who is always getting into fights on the playground is a pupil with Asperger's syndrome, who needs help in acquiring social skills, or when the extreme clumsiness and tendency to bump into people and break objects is not from carelessness or rudeness, but happens when someone has severe dyspraxia. Apart from anything else, a diagnosis may act as a fast track to getting some form of support. Children who have a statement of SEN, for instance, will have the provision that is needed set out as part of the documentation.

Disadvantages of labelling

Turning now to the disadvantages of labelling, there is a danger that a label can become a self-fulfilling prophecy. If a particular diagnosis is attached to a child, so the argument runs, others will expect a certain pattern of behaviour and that behaviour may increase. It may even mean that parents or staff take the attitude that the child cannot help it and must therefore be excused for behaving in this way. This is very different from making allowances for the pupil. Furthermore, those who work with the child, whether at home or at school, may focus too much on the label and see the child in terms of their category of need, instead of first and foremost as a person who happens to have a particular condition.

Another disadvantage may be that it leads to an unnecessary concern about how the child will develop, because parents or teachers may lack the understanding that there will be a continuum, from those who are mildly affected to those who are severely affected, for the majority of disorders. Along with this concern may go a lowering of expectations, rather than working with the child to help him or her progress despite any problems. In schools, staff may see pupils with particular labels as being outside their expertise and the responsibility of specialist staff, rather than the responsibility being shared. This attitude may be encouraged by professionals using medical and psychological jargon, which can be intimidating to others who are not familiar with the terminology. Although some children and young people, such as Chris Mitchell, are relieved by being given an explanation for their difficulties, others may resent being different and a label emphasises this difference. They may also use their condition as an excuse for not trying, rather than work harder to overcome any obstacles to progress.

As has been shown, labelling is not always accurate, so this could be seen as another reason for not labelling children at all, particularly when there is a growing realisation that categories of need are not as discrete as once thought, but can overlap and also frequently co-exist. If having one diagnosis can be damaging, what is the effect of having two or three? Then there are the individuals who clearly have problems of some kind, but who fail to fit neatly into any of the categories that are recognised at present, leading to a lack of support for them. Table 3.1. gives a summary of some of the points that have been raised about labelling.

While it can be argued that diagnostic labels stigmatise a child and move the focus from seeing the child as an individual to focusing on the label itself, a label does not necessarily mean that a person's individuality is removed. As Victoria Biggs says in the foreword to her book, *Caged in Chaos*, 'Use the label but don't be defined by it' (2005: 9).

Table 3.1   The advantages and disadvantages of labelling

Advantages	Disadvantages
Helps child to understand nature of his/her difficulties	Gives child an excuse for not trying
Helps teachers to understand child's difficulties	Adult expectations of child may be lowered
Helps parents to know it is not their fault	Parents may feel negative about the prognosis
May attract specialist resources and support	Moves the focus from a person to a label
Makes it easier to target interventions and resources more effectively	May result in non-specialist staff feeling disempowered
May make it easier for child to work with those who have similar needs	Labels can be imprecise or wrong
Child less likely to be excluded if nature of difficulties is known	Label becomes a self-fulfilling prophecy
Parents and child may have access to support groups	Child resents being 'different'
Child accepted by peers, who make allowances for his/her difficulties	People do not fit neatly into the categories invented for them

 Questions for reflection

1   What do you think is the main advantage and disadvantage of labelling a child?

2   From your experience, can you recall an example of a label being a significant advantage and/or disadvantage to the person concerned?

3   Overall, do you believe that the advantages outweigh the disadvantages or not?

Complications and controversies of labelling

Labels on their own are not much use. They are only helpful if they act as a guide as to the kind of support the child needs. The importance in getting the label right lies in the fact that the diagnosis should lead on to some kind of intervention. This may range from something as simple as allowing a child with dyslexia extra time to complete tasks, to creating a designated area of a classroom for a young child with ASD.

There is sometimes a danger that once a diagnosis of a particular disorder has been made, the professional making the diagnosis may not investigate any further. This means that while the main presenting condition will be identified, any other difficulties may be overlooked. This may reduce the effectiveness of any intervention, for instance in the way the child is taught, because the teacher will lack the bigger picture. In Martin Kutscher's book, *Kids in the Syndrome Mix of ADHD, LD, Asperger's, Tourette's, Bipolar, and More*, he suggests that 'Co-occurrence of multiple difficulties is the norm, not the exception' (2005: 11).

An example of a recent book that covers a similar range of difficulties, yet does not take account of new insights into the origins of neurodevelopmental disorders, is

Robin Pauc's *Is That My Child?* The strapline of *Exploding the myths of Dyspraxia, Dyslexia, Tourette's syndrome, ADD, ADHD and OCD* gives a flavour of the direction the book takes. He puts forward the idea that all humans are born before their brains are fully developed and before a particular type of neurons known as **spindle cells** have appeared. Pauc speculates that in autism, spindle cells are absent altogether and are under-functioning in the other disorders, which he terms **developmental delay syndrome**.

Pauc's claim that humans are born prematurely has been discussed since the 1920s. As the brain is not the only organ that could be considered to be underdeveloped at birth, this idea cannot serve as a framework for labelling neurodevelopmental disorders as one common condition. Nor does it answer the question as to why the majority of people do not suffer from any of these disorders despite being born 'prematurely.'

Although cutting down the number of labels in this way would counteract the growing number of terms coming into use, it is not a credible solution. As mentioned earlier, at one time *dyslexia* was used almost synonymously with the term *specific learning difficulties*, as it was the only kind of SpLD that was commonly discussed. Although there may be a query as to how far dyslexia, dyspraxia, dyscalculia and dysgraphia should be seen as four separate disorders, Brian Butterworth, one of the leading experts on dyscalculia, points out that, despite an overlap of symptoms, there are, for instance, children with dyslexia who are not dyscalculic, and those with dyscalculia who are not dyslexic.

Dyslexia has the longest history of the four types of SpLD being discussed, yet, in the last couple of years, there has been some controversy around the label, with Julian Elliott, a psychologist and researcher, querying whether or not it is a 'myth.' Although this had a great deal of media coverage, it seems likely that at the root of Elliott's concerns is the view that the term has been used so widely as a label, that it is either meaningless or is in danger of becoming so. There are many different reasons why children have difficulty learning to read (which, after all, is not a natural process like starting to talk or walk). They may have delayed language development, which has a knock-on effect on their ability to become literate; they may have poor auditory or visual discrimination skills, which makes it harder for them to hear the sounds in words or to discriminate between similar-looking words on the page; they may have difficulties with memory; or they may simply not be ready to learn to read at the age dictated by educational policies.

Listening carefully to the arguments, it is not so much that there is disagreement about whether or not dyslexia exists, but about acknowledging that, within a wider group of poor readers, a much smaller percentage has a neurological condition that results in dyslexia. These are the children who are particularly resistant to remediation and who may only make progress when regular (preferably daily) practice and instruction are available from skilled and knowledgeable adults. There are also likely to be family members who have had similar or related difficulties.

The controversy about dyslexia highlights another more general problem with labelling, that of knowing when to give a child a diagnosis. SEN itself is a continuum, from those with long-term, severe difficulties at one end, to those with mild and possibly temporary difficulties at the other. Within the SEN continuum, the developmental disorders under discussion in this book have their own continuum from mild to severe. At the less severe end of any continuum, there will not be a clear demarcation between those who are given a label and those who are not. In the first chapter of this book, reference was made to the autistic spectrum and to the fact that PDD-NOS or atypical autism, are terms that are given when a child has some of the symptoms of autism, but not sufficient for a full diagnosis to be made. In other conditions, there may be no halfway house, so a child either has ADHD, or s/he does not. As all human beings are unique, there will be some who fit neatly into categories and some who fail to do so, including those who seem to have features of a number of different disorders without having enough symptoms in any one category to be given a diagnosis of anything. Michael Farrell, in his book *Special Educational Needs* sums this up as follows:

> It is not assumed that each category of mental disorder is completely discrete, with 'absolute' boundaries separating the disorder from other mental disorders or from an absence of mental disorder. (2004:72)

Farrell raises two points here: the question of where a disorder shades into normality, and where one disorder shades into another. The more that is discovered about neurodevelopmental disorders, the more overlap there seems to be in the symptoms they share. This has led to a number of books appearing in recent years, where a particular symptom has been decribed that goes across a number of disorders. For instance, in *Understanding Sensory Dysfunction* by Emmons and Anderson (2005), the authors describe sensory dysfunction and then relate it to some of the conditions in which it may appear, including ASD, ADHD and SpLD. Similarly, Kurtz's (2008) book on *Understanding Motor Skills in Children with Dyspraxia, ADHD, Autism and Other Learning Disabilities* takes a similar approach.

Another complication of labelling is the way developmental disorders are described in different countries. For instance, in Scandinavia, the term DAMP is used for children who appear to have a combination of ADHD and Developmental Coordination Disorder (dyspraxia). DAMP stands for **d**eficits in **a**ttention, **m**otor control and **p**erception. It is interesting to note that ADHD and dyspraxia are seen to go together sufficiently often to warrant one label.

In America, NVLD (non-verbal learning disorders) is a recognised term (although it does not appear in DSM-IV-TR). The same condition is sometimes referred to as *right hemisphere learning disorder*, as the symptoms of difficulties with motor skills, social skills, sensory and visuospatial problems are largely right hemisphere activities. The National Autistic Society (NAS) sees NVLD/right hemisphere learning disorder as being included within the definition of Asperger's syndrome, with no need for it to be recognised separately.

 Questions for reflection

1   Can you think of any children or young people you know who have puzzled you because their difficulties do not fall into a particular category? Do you think they might have either more than one condition, or might they be one of those individuals who have symptoms of more than one disorder, but insufficient to provide any diagnosis?

2   Have you come across anyone with more than one kind of specific learning difficulty? If so, what combination did s/he have and how did it affect him or her?

The rise and rise of labelling

Despite the Warnock Committee in 1978 introducing the term 'special educational needs', which was in part an attempt to move away from labelling children, the number of labels has actually increased as more conditions and syndromes have been recognised. As well as the different types of SpLD mentioned previously, other groups that have expanded considerably are ADHD and ASD. In the case of the former, children who might have been considered overactive and disobedient may now be given the label ADHD. Formal education is starting at an earlier age, and boys, in particular, who like being active, may display symptoms of ADHD simply because they are not ready to sit down and be taught. This is a case where adjusting the environment, rather than labelling the child, may be relevant to some individuals.

Autism might be said to have risen exponentially, from one in a thousand or more being identified a decade ago, to the incidence now being quoted as around one in 90. Some of the reasons for the growth in identification are apparent. Firstly, ASD takes in a much wider group of children than those who are classically autistic. There is general agreement, for instance, that Asperger's syndrome is part of the autistic spectrum. Secondly, paediatricians and other professionals are far more skilled at recognising the condition and differentiating it from other disorders. Thirdly, while ASD may have a neurological basis, other elements in the environment act as triggers in those who are susceptible. Although it is not known what these triggers might be, there have been massive changes to the environment, and the number of triggers would appear to have multiplied. It may not be dangerous for most people to eat chemically laden food, breathe polluted air or be surrounded by technological aids exuding radio waves, but for a few vulnerable individuals, it may be.

The two brief case studies that follow have been designed to give an illustration of the current breadth of the autistic spectrum. Gerry is a child who would always have been viewed as having autism and he represents the pupil that few teachers would have difficulty in picking out as autistic. Paul, however, is typical of a child who might not have been given a diagnosis before the term 'autism' was extended to those who have Asperger's syndrome.

 Case study 3.1: Gerry, 4 years old

Gerry was diagnosed as autistic when he was three years old. His parents had realised something was wrong from a very early stage. Although he looked 'normal' at birth and his parents were thrilled with their firstborn son, they soon became concerned that he did not seem to react to them. His mother watched the way that other mothers and babies interacted and tried desperately to get Gerry to respond to her smiles or to her comforting arms. But Gerry did not want to be held and showed no interest in the rattle she shook in front of him, in an effort to gain his attention and interest.

Shortly after he was four, Gerry started at the local nursery school, but he upset the other children with his constant screaming. He did not want to play with any of the activities that were set out, except for the sand tray, where he would run the sand through his fingers incessantly. The staff tried to interest him in filling little pails with sand and making sandcastles, but he ignored their efforts, or became annoyed when they invaded his space, and started screaming. Gerry had no speech and did not respond when his name was called. He seemed to live in a world of his own and showed no interest in the other children.

 Case study 3.2: Paul, 10 years old

Paul, on the other hand, did not receive a diagnosis until he was 10. His parents thought of him as a difficult child who found it hard to play with other children without squabbling. On the other hand, they were very proud of his obvious intelligence. Paul was passionate about cars. He knew the different makes and where they came from by their number plates. He and his dad would have earnest discussions about the finer points of the latest model on the market. In fact, his interest in cars dominated his life and he had few other interests. He had no friends, as they were put off by his talking at them about cars rather than showing any signs of wanting to converse with them about their interests. To them, he seemed very self-centred. His parents were concerned that he would have great difficulty in fitting in at secondary schools. That was when he received his diagnosis.

Labelling put into perspective

While there are problems with labelling and mistakes will occur, this does not mean that diagnosing children's difficulties, including neurodevelopmental disorders, is either unimportant or unnecessary. In the majority of cases, children will be given the right diagnosis and that diagnosis will help to steer those who are concerned with their education and welfare to understand more about how their needs might be met in the most appropriate manner.

Labels may be seen as having both positive and negative attributes, but, in effect, a diagnosis is the first step towards helping those who are involved with the child to be better informed about the approach that may be most effective. But however many labels a child has, the important aspect is to focus on children as individuals, and to work out how best to help them to make progress. Everyone has strengths and weaknesses, and finds some subjects or areas of learning harder than others. In children with developmental disorders, the weaknesses may be more exaggerated and harder to overcome, because of the underlying causes. This does not mean, however, that they cannot be helped to improve. The more that is discovered about the brain, the more evident it becomes that it can respond flexibly and that it can go on increasing its ability to learn.

In addition to highlighting likely areas of difficulty, a label can also reveal where a child's strengths might lie: the child with ADHD can have enormous enthusiasm and energy, provided that it can be channelled; the individual with ASD (depending on the extent of any learning difficulties), can have unusual powers of concentration, an eye for detail, and an excellent rote memory; while both those with ASD and those with SpLD may have visual strengths, including the ability to think three-dimensionally.

The skill in teaching pupils with SEN lies in making them confident learners, and building on their strengths while supporting them in overcoming any barriers to their learning. Any label should not detract from the recognition that all children and young people, whether or not they have a disorder, will have their own distinct and distinctive personalities and this will play a part in how they respond to any difficulties they have and any interventions that are offered.

The plethora of labels now in existence and the widening way in which they are used has already been mentioned, but there can be the opposite problem as well. Parents, in particular, query whether, in some cases, labels are used enough, or whether some local authorities (LAs) are failing to recognise certain conditions, because they do not have the provision to meet the needs. The link between recognition of a condition and the provision for it is an important one. While society has a responsibility to provide the resources, so that social institutions are able to guarantee at least adequate support, resources are always likely to be finite. If support is going to continue to depend on certain labels being acquired, some children and young people are going to miss out.

It is possible that some sort of crossroads will be reached in terms of labelling. Not only are the additional labels being used creating some confusion, but, increasingly, children are being given more than one label. There is a lack of clarity about whether all these separate labels are necessary, or whether some of them are simply descriptions of symptoms already identified as being part of a condition the child is already known to have. It is a fairly recent phenomenon for children to be described as having co-existing disorders, yet the four main groups of disorders under discussion have been shown to co-exist with each other, as well as with other disorders. If labels continue to multiply and the numbers of children with co-existing disorders continues to increase, a new approach might have to be taken, which focuses on the symptoms, so that each one of these can be addressed, regardless of any labels.

This is the approach that is taken in the next chapter, when strategies are listed under the types of difficulty children may have, rather than under named disorders. This is not meant to detract from the fact that diagnostic labels, however inadequate or difficult to get right, will continue to play an important role in the education and care of those who have SEN for the foreseeable future. Undoubtedly, there is a balance to be had between overdiagnosis on the one hand and underdiagnosis on the other, but this is not a reason for saying that the whole notion of giving children and young people diagnostic labels should be abandoned. The shift in recent years from placing children in categories to giving them a descriptive label has been a healthy one. Time will tell what the next step will be.

Summary

Although labelling can be a partial and inaccurate process, at present it is still the best way of getting the information on which to base the kind of help a child needs.

Diagnosis may depend on the experience and training of the professional undertaking the assessment. It is always preferable for professionals from different disciplines, plus the school and the family, to be involved in contributing to a diagnosis of any complexity.

In addition to its imprecision, and the disadvantages as well as the advantages, labelling can assist our understanding of the implications of an identified condition.

The most important aspect is to focus, first and foremost, on the child as an individual, regardless of any label or labels he or she may have been given.

Further Reading

Blakemore-Brown, L. (2002) *Reweaving the Autistic Tapestry: Autism, Asperger's Syndrome and ADHD*. London: Jessica Kingsley.

Kurtz, L.A. (2008) *Understanding Motor Skills in Children with Dyspraxia, ADHD, Autism and Other Learning Disabilities*. London: Jessica Kingsley.

Kutscher, M.L. (2005) *Kids in the Syndrome Mix of ADHD, LD, Asperger's Tourette's, Bipolar and More!* London: Jessica Kingsley.

Mitchell, C. (2005) *Glass Half Empty: Glass Half Full: How Asperger's Syndrome Changed My Life*. London: Paul Chapman Publishing.

4

Dealing with different disorders in the classroom

> **This chapter moves away from labels to focus on:**
> - **how children's thinking develops**
> - **different intelligences and learning styles**
> - **common areas of difficulty that go across the developmental disorders being discussed**
> - **the importance of maintaining motivation and self-esteem**
> - **practical strategies for supporting pupils in overcoming the difficulties they encounter.**

Attitudes to children's learning

Following on from the chapters on how the brain learns and the usefulness or otherwise of giving children labels, this chapter focuses on what can be done to assist those who find learning difficult. The approach taken is that while knowing the nature of pupils' difficulties is an important starting point for helping them, the next step is to shift the focus to knowing what aspects of learning they find hard. This approach will make it possible to include those who have:

- obvious difficulties but no clear diagnosis

- a firm diagnosis of a single condition

- more than one diagnostic label.

In the same way that TV cooks see it as part of their role to talk about how the digestion works, and sports coaches tell their players about how their muscles work, teachers should interest themselves in how the brain works. This will enable them to be better informed about how to teach, as well as helping them to explain to their pupils how they learn.

There are some instances where what schools are being asked to do runs counter to what is known about child development. For instance, in this country there is an emphasis on becoming literate at a very young age. Yet it is known that the fine finger coordination necessary for writing often does not develop until after the age of five, and that boys are slower to develop this skill than girls. Boys, in particular, may enjoy a more active style of learning and sitting them down to explore the mysteries of phonics may not be the best way to encourage them to become lifelong readers. Teaching must coincide with physiological and psychological readiness to be effective, otherwise there is a danger that children can spend hours of their lives being taught something they are not ready to learn.

The development of thinking skills

Brains are built to soak up any opportunity for learning, so all children should be seen as being active participants in the learning process regardless of their basic level of intelligence.

Before turning to look at strategies to help pupils learn, it is useful to keep in mind how children's thinking develops. In the last century, the ideas of the French biologist, Jean Piaget (1896–1980) were very influential. He speculated there were certain times when there is acceleration in thinking and suggested that these transitions take place at approximately 18 months, 7 years, and 11 or 12 years, with children passing through sensorimotor, pre-operational, concrete operational and formal operational stages of thought.

Lev Vygotsky (1896–1934), the Russian psychologist, took the view that social interaction plays a fundamental role in the development of **cognition**. His idea of the *zone of proximal development* (which is the area between what a child can already accomplish, and what he or she can achieve with the guidance of a more knowledgeable person) has had a resurgence recently. Later Jerome Bruner, the American psychologist, was also influenced by Vygotsky. Bruner saw both environmental and experiential factors contributing to intellectual ability. He based his ideas about development on the role of categorisation and its importance in helping children to make sense of the world.

Current knowledge suggests that children start by thinking in terms of the here and now. They learn to problem solve by gaining information from the senses as they explore their environment. When they begin to use language to name and represent objects, their thinking is able to become detached from firsthand experience. Another aspect of their cognitive development is evident in the way that they learn to categorise, moving from classifying objects by single features to appreciating that the same objects can be categorised in different ways. As their powers of reasoning increase, they develop a sense of self, the ability to hold several aspects of a problem in mind, to understand the need to take turns and that people can have different perspectives. They are able to think logically about concrete objects and to understand cause and effect. Next, they move on to abstract thought, finally being able to think about their own thinking (known as metacognition).

Different intelligences, learning styles and attributes

Another aspect of learning is Howard Gardner's notion of different intelligences, which he developed in order to move away from the idea that intelligence could be treated as a single entity, capable of being reduced to one measurement known as the intelligence quotient (IQ).

Gardner started by identifying seven types of intelligence, to which he later added an eighth and then a ninth.

> ## 🔑 Key point Gardner's intelligences
>
> | | |
> |---|---|
> | verbal-linguistic | good at talking, listening, reading and writing |
> | logical-mathematical | good at mathematics and reasoning |
> | spatial | good spatial awareness |
> | kinaesthetic | good at physical skills and movement |
> | interpersonal | good at relationships; empathetic |
> | intrapersonal | self-aware; able to think and act independently |
> | musical | good sense of melody and rhythm |
> | naturalistic | in tune with the environment |
> | aesthetic | having an appreciation of colours, shapes, textures and scents |

Since then, Gardner has written a book called *Five Minds for the Future* (2006). In it, he describes the minds that will be needed for learning in the twenty-first century, namely:

- discipline

- synthesis

- creativity

- respect

- ethics.

It will be fascinating to see how far his latest ideas influence education. However, it was as a result of his notion of **multiple intelligences** that an interest in different learning styles developed and the importance of flexibility in teaching was appreciated.

During the last decade or so, there has also been considerable interest in how far people have a preference for learning in different ways, which is sometimes referred to as 'VAK': visual, auditory and kinaesthetic styles of learning. 'Tactile' is sometimes included within the term 'kinaesthetic,' but there is a case for adding it to the list, as the two terms are distinct from each other.

Key point Sensory styles of learning

'VAKT' learners prefer:

visual	visually presented information
auditory	information that is heard
kinaesthetic	being actively involved through physical movement
tactile	using the sense of touch

There is a debate about how far it is helpful to think in terms of pupils being VAKT learners. While there is no doubt that people vary in the ways in which they like to learn, it is also the case that different types of learning call for different styles, so that all these styles need to be utilised in order to maximise pupils' learning potential. Therefore, it is helpful to present learners with information presented in different ways and to allow them to respond in a variety of modes, rather than simply labelling people as visual, auditory, kinaesthetic or tactile learners.

Another way of looking at how to help learners is to take the approach of the psychologist Guy Claxton. Instead of focusing on the basic intellectual skills of the 3Rs of reading, writing and arithmetic, he has concentrated on the attributes the learner needs to develop (Claxton, 2002). He says that the 4Rs needed by pupils today are:

1 Resilience: knowing how to stick to a task

2 Resourcefulness: knowing how to explore different ways of achieving a task

3 Reflectiveness: being able to reflect on one's own learning

4 Reciprocity: being able to learn with others as well as by oneself.

These attributes may not come easily to pupils with developmental disorders, yet it may be particularly important for them to learn to persevere, to develop a variety of strategies and to be able to think about how they learn.

〰️ **Questions for reflection**

1 Do you think that Gardner was right in suggesting there are different types of intelligence, and, if so, do you agree with his list?

2 How would you apply this to children with complex conditions?

3 What is your own attitude to VAKT? Is it the same as the approach taken by your school?

4 Do you agree with Claxton's 4Rs, and, if so, what difference does it or should it make to your teaching?

Areas for development

It will have become apparent by now that there are areas of difficulty that go across the neurodevelopmental disorders under discussion. The brain needs to coordinate these functions, all of which, in various combinations, may be problematic in certain disorders:

- motivation

- attention

- organisation

- memory

- motor skills

- communication

- literacy

- numeracy

- socialisation.

Whilst each of these areas is considered in turn and strategies suggested for helping children and young people to overcome any difficulties they are experiencing, it is recognised that many of the areas overlap.

Although literacy is part of communication, it is considered separately because of its importance as a school subject.

Motivation

Motivation is addressed first because building up their self-esteem is one of the key tasks of those involved in the education of pupils who find learning difficult. Otherwise, they are in danger of becoming unmotivated, because of repeatedly experiencing what they perceive to be failure. Yet, it is particularly important for those with neurodevelopmental disorders to develop resilience, so that they will be prepared to practise and to consolidate their learning, until new connections are established in the brain. There are two kinds of motivation: extrinsic motivation and intrinsic motivation. Usually, the former will lead to the latter.

 Key points Motivation

Extrinsic motivation

Learners need some outside driver or reward to encourage them to learn. This might simply be praise, or a more tangible reward, such as being able to choose an activity, being allowed out first at break time, or being given a merit card or sweet.

Intrinsic motivation

Learners are self-motivated and do not need any external rewards. They feel an inward sense or drive to accomplish a task. They understand what they want to achieve and how to achieve it. They enjoy the learning experience. The very act of learning is its own reward.

Figure 4.1   Strategies for improving motivation, confidence and self-esteem

- Teach pupils that making mistakes is part of the road to success, so that they become more resilient and do not give up easily.

- Keep tasks short and make sure they are achievable, so that success rather than failure becomes the pattern.

- Give frequent praise and rewards, while keeping in mind what motivates different pupils and the manner in which they prefer to receive praise.

- Avoid getting into a downward spiral of negativity by keeping in mind the ability of the brain to grow new connections.

- Treat each day as a fresh opportunity to work on behavioural issues and wipe the slate clean.

- Explain to pupils that the brain improves with exercise: the more they try to learn, the better at learning they will become.

- Build on pupils' strengths, abilities and interests by providing different ways of tackling tasks, including a choice of how they present their homework.

- Give immediate feedback where possible, emphasising any achievement and conveying a sense of enthusiasm about the learning that still needs to take place.

- If there is not time to give pupils immediate feedback, find moments to discuss any comments on their work so that they are clear what they need to do to improve.

- Incorporate computers and other multimedia resources into activities and lessons as much as possible.

- Discuss goals so pupils have a sense of purpose and something to aim for.

- Demonstrate how teachers have to learn too, and reinforce the message that everyone is on a journey of lifelong learning, not just those who are students in school.

- Make sure pupils know how much their success means to those who teach and support them, and that staff have confidence in their ability to succeed.

 Photocopiable:

Educating Children with Complex Conditions © Winand H. Dittrich and Rona Tutt, 2008.

Not only must pupils with recognised conditions be prepared to work as hard as their peers, it might well be that they will need to work harder. If success keeps eluding them despite the efforts they make, it is easy to see why they may feel like giving up. Thomas Edison may have been able to recognise that the hundreds of attempts it took him to produce the light bulb were all steps on the road to success, but few pupils with SEN would have the confidence or resilience to see it in this way. Rather, they may feel it is easier not to try than to risk another failure. Teachers and others working with pupils who have SEN need to be very aware of the importance of maintaining pupils' morale, to remain positive themselves, and to keep reminding their pupils that they can and will learn, even if some tasks are hard for them. Motivation is a prime mover in achievement; all pupils need to feel a sense of purpose if they are going to try to succeed at a task. Experiencing success will build up the confidence and self-esteem that will feed into maintaining motivation.

Attention

Pupils are often reprimanded for not paying attention, yet for some, this is a genuine area of difficulty. Children with ADHD and those with ASD, for instance, can be overwhelmed by an overload of information.

 Key points The senses and perceptual difficulties

The senses

Normally, the sense organs pick up information, so that it can be processed (**sensation**). (In the case of people who have a visual or hearing impairment, the sense organs or the pathways to the brain are impaired.) Perception is involved when people become aware of receiving sensory information.

Perceptual difficulties

These are caused when the right information is available (that is to say that there is no visual or hearing impairment), but either the brain's mechanism for integrating and processing the information from different parts of the brain is faulty, or there are problems within a particular sense modality.

Perceptual sensitivity

Some children suffer from being hypersensitive (oversensitive) or hyposensitive (lack normal levels of sensitivity), due to a failure in the workings of the frontal brain.

Children with ASD, in particular, may be either hypersensitive or hyposensitive to visual or auditory input, as well as to taste, touch and smell. This makes it very hard for them to concentrate, either because they are overwhelmed, or because the information they are receiving does not make enough impact. In addition, they often

Figure 4.2 Strategies for improving attention skills

- Use pupils' names and draw their attention to what they need to look at or listen to.

- Make classes orderly but exciting places to be.

- Include novelty in lessons to capture attention and imagination, whether in the style of the lesson, the content, the resources used, or where it takes place, including outdoors.

- Break up lessons into different activities, so that listening will be interspersed with opportunities to talk and to move about.

- Think of ways of making lessons multisensory and interactive, so that pupils have visual and auditory information, as well as being able to handle objects and be active.

- Balance the amount of teacher and pupil talk – pupils learn through expressing their ideas and discussing them with others.

- Provide opportunities for pupils to exercise. This can be from a few stretching movements at their desks to intervals for a short workout.

- Allow opportunities to drink water or have a snack.

- Do not insist on eye contact if it makes a pupil uncomfortable, but allow them to be at a distance if they show they can learn this way. Some pupils prefer to work standing up.

- Be flexible and allow 'concentrators'. Use favourite objects/activities as rewards.

- Work out very gradual steps for desensitising pupils who are hypersensitive.

- Seat highly distractible pupils at the front or give them their own space within the classroom, screened off from distractions.

- Allow pupils who need it to go to a 'time out' room or area, or to have additional short breaks, to prevent them feeling overwhelmed or out of control.

 Photocopiable:
Educating Children with Complex Conditions © Winand H. Dittrich and Rona Tutt, 2008.

have difficulty in integrating the information they receive, as they focus on the detail rather than the completeness of the information they receive through the senses.

There may be other reasons why a child appears to be inattentive. They may find it hard to sit still or to listen for as long as expected. They may not understand the content of a lesson and so they switch off. Paradoxically, giving children who need it something to manipulate while listening does not distract them, but acts as a 'concentrator' (which is what some of them are called). This is similar to adults doodling while listening or thinking. It is also thought that the movement may help by activating the motor cortex, making it more receptive to incoming information.

Organisation

Difficulties with organisational skills goes across all the disorders under discussion. It includes difficulties with planning and sequencing, as well as being able to respond flexibly to change. These areas are under the control of the executive function, which is in the frontal and pre-frontal cortex of the brain. Because these pupils may be struggling to make sense of their surroundings and the learning they are being asked to do, they may appear very disorganised, wandering around in a 'sea of unknowing,' and failing to get to grips with reality. Although it will take time and patience on the part of both staff and pupils, organisational skills can be taught and will improve if sufficient guidance is offered and children practise the routines that will help them to become more self-aware. Organising behaviour is to a large degree finding the right information to make the right decisions. In its widest sense, organisation may encompass:

- being self-aware and able to make choices

- understanding cause and effect in terms of both the environment and the consequence of any actions taken

- being able to decide on which is the right course of action

- being ready to learn: in the right place, at the right time, with the necessary equipment

- being able to think ahead, set goals and plan for the future

- having the flexibility to adjust to changing circumstances, rather than keeping to a pre-conceived plan (perseveration).

Younger children may have particular difficulties in this area, as the frontal cortex continues to develop well into adolescence. This may be one reason why children with ADHD, in particular, seem to become less impulsive and to find it easier to curb inappropriate behaviour as they grow older.

Memory

The importance of memory cannot be over emphasised, as learning and memory are inseparable. Chapter 2 gave some details about the different types of memory

Figure 4.3 Strategies for organisation

- Set a good example by keeping a well organised classroom which makes it easy for pupils to find what they need.

- Encourage pupils to keep their desks and possessions tidy.

- Have clear rules and routines, so that pupils know what the expectations are for the lesson.

- Help pupils to understand the sequence of the day by providing visual or written individual timetables, as well as class timetables.

- Ask pupils questions about what they need to take home or bring to school.

- Discuss with them what strategies they will use to remind themselves what they need to do.

- Encourage pupils to have the equipment they need for each lesson on their desks at the start of the session.

- Check pupils' understanding of the homework they have been set. Ask them to repeat back what they have to do.

- Use homework diaries and discuss with pupils how to prioritise their work: when to do it and when it needs to be handed in.

- Make sure they know what the objectives are for each lesson and help them to think about whether or not they have been achieved.

- Give 'either/or' choices before working up to a greater degree of choice.

- Provide a starting point for creative writing rather than a blank sheet of paper.

- Help them to structure stories and essays by drawing the sequence of events in pictures first, or by writing one key sentence for each of the paragraphs they will be using. In either case, this will help them to think about having a beginning, middle and end.

- Build the idea of flexibility into their thinking, so that they learn to cope with the unexpected.

Photocopiable:

Educating Children with Complex Conditions © Winand H. Dittrich and Rona Tutt, 2008.

that make up the system for storing and recalling information. It is not always realised that the working memory lasts for only a matter of seconds or minutes, with a maximum of two minutes thought to be the longest that something is remembered, if it is not rehearsed or reinforced in some way. Despite the overriding importance of memory, little attention is paid in schools as to how to help pupils improve their ability to memorise information. This is an area where a lack of knowledge about the brain has resulted in staff and their students missing an opportunity to increase learning capacity. It is common for pupils with neurodevelopmental disorders to have memory problems, although there are exceptions, such as the strong rote learning ability of those with ASD.

Part of the difficulties of children with SLI are thought to lie in the area of memory. The working memory (see Chapter 2) enables people to store and manipulate information at the same time. Individuals with SLI may find it hard to follow what is said if the language is complex or the information is too lengthy. They also have difficulty holding that information in their heads while they try to respond to what has been said, either by carrying out a task or by making a verbal response. Difficulty in retrieving the words they want to use is also a feature of SLI and is part of the memory system. Teachers can help these pupils by not using unnecessarily complicated wording.

Pupils with neurodevelopmental disorders in general may need more time to process information, to make sense of new concepts and to practise new skills. Information that is only half understood is less likely to be recalled, so linking new skills to prior knowledge, as well as learning the same concepts in different ways are both important. As well as the variety this affords, it is also the case that kinaesthetic and tactile feedback and being actively involved enhances memory. In order to be stored or to become automatic, skills have to be practised over and over again for a long period of time. Skills that have not been practised for long enough will not become automatic. Periods of learning, interspersed with short bursts of activity, allow the child time to process the information and improve the likelihood of it being remembered, because the learning is broken up into shorter chunks. 'Chunking' information (which is what people do when trying to remember telephone numbers), is a proven strategy for increasing the amount of information that can be memorised.

Motor skills

The role of movement in helping children to learn has been recognised for some time. In the early years, this is seen by their progress after starting to sit up, to crawl, to stand and then to walk. The coordination involved in these activities helps to form connections between the two halves of the brain, and so facilitates learning more generally. Impairments in the cerebellum can lead to difficulties in coordinating movement, in balancing, and a whole range of activities that rely on the coordination of movements. Children experiencing difficulties with gross motor skills are likely to have difficulty with fine motor skills as well.

Figure 4.4   Strategies for helping memory

- Keep sentences short to reduce unnecessary complexity, particularly when content is unfamiliar to pupils.

- Avoid overloading the memory by expecting pupils to both hold and manipulate information at the same time.

- Teach new concepts by repeating the key words so that pupils have a better chance of absorbing the information.

- Attach new knowledge to previous learning, so that pupils build on what they already know.

- Give pupils sufficient time to process what they have been told and check their understanding. Allow sufficient time for them to think about and organise their answers.

- Plan lessons so that the same concepts are put across in different ways, for instance, linking oral information with visual cues.

- Link material to be learnt with actions: gestures, singing, or using rhythm, as using the body heightens awareness and increases memory.

- Provide sufficient opportunities for repetition, practice and consolidating learning.

- Find ways of encouraging pupils to use their initiative, so that activities become more significant to them and are easier to remember.

- Provide support for pupils with word-retrieval problems by giving them clues to finding the word. Give practise in recalling the same words, so they become easier to retrieve.

- Encourage word association games to develop word-finding skills.

- Chunk information to be remembered, so that there is not so much to remember at a stretch.

- Talk pupils through their role in events, before, during and after they occur, in order to increase self-awareness and support the declarative and autobiographical memory.

- Talk to pupils about memory and help them to recognise the strategies that help them, including visualisation.

Photocopiable:

Educating Children with Complex Conditions © Winand H. Dittrich and Rona Tutt, 2008.

Key points Motor skills

Gross motor

Gross motor skills involve being able to use the larger muscle groups, for instance to walk and run, and to throw and catch a ball.

Fine motor

Fine motor skills are involved in activities like pencil control, eating with a knife and fork, doing up buttons and manipulating construction kits.

Balance

An underdeveloped sense of balance will mean a child has difficulty standing on one leg, walking along a narrow beam, or being slow to learn to ride a bike.

The frontal cortex is involved in motor memory, while the basal ganglia and hippocampus store memories of similar movements being used in the past. When movements are practised and refined in order to perfect a skill, more neurons become involved. Recently, **mirror neurons** have been discovered. These are neurons that are activated by watching others perform movements. This means that it is possible to improve motor skills by watching others as well as by practising these same skills. This opens up new possibilities for helping pupils with problems in this area. The development of 'virtual reality' computerised games, for instance of football matches where the players can be manipulated, is also an area to explore.

As well as breaking up the school day with periods of activity, pupils also need periods of rest from being taught. This allows time for readjustment and readiness for the next spell of learning.

Communication

As mentioned in the opening chapter (see page 13), communication covers both spoken and written communication, as well as gestures and signs, which should be seen as important aspects of communication in the classroom. They support the meaning of the language being used (by pointing or gesticulating), as well as being a means of communication (as in the case of Makaton or British Sign Language).

Being able to communicate, both in terms of 'reading' people emotionally and having the language to understand and exchange ideas is crucial to learning, as is the need to have the words with which to build up concepts and employ higher thinking skills. So communication covers:

Figure 4.5   Strategies for helping with motor skills

- Break down motor skills tasks into their component parts and practise each stage separately.

- Remind pupils that the more they take part in physical activities the more skilled they will become.

- Use a variety of different sized balls, balloons and bats to practise ball skills.

- Programme short bursts of activity into the day and into lessons. Start the day with a 10-minute workout for the pupils who need it.

- Make pupils aware that activity increases the supply of oxygen to the brain and strengthens neural connections.

- Make sure chairs are the right height relative to the desk, with younger pupils having their feet firmly planted on the floor.

- If fine motor skills are poor, check whether there is a problem with gross motor skills and work on these as well if necessary.

- Have a variety of different sized pencils, pencil grips and pens for pupils to try.

- Teach handwriting by using different materials: writing in the air, in sand, in foam and using sandpaper letters.

- Reinforce the skill of handwriting by giving daily practice at the primary stage, making sure that incorrect habits are not being reinforced, but are being corrected

- Provide opportunities for those with severe difficulties to learn touch-typing and allow the use of laptops where available.

- Supply younger pupils with specially adapted cutlery and non-skid mats for plates.

- Have ridged rulers or ones with knobs pupils can hold.

- Try book rests or angle boards for pupils who move their heads or bodies across the desk to read or write.

 Photocopiable:

Educating Children with Complex Conditions © Winand H. Dittrich and Rona Tutt, 2008.

- listening

- emotions and gestures

- oracy

- reading

- writing.

As this area includes so much that is fundamental to learning at school, literacy skills are dealt with under a separate heading although they are part of communication.

There is an obvious link between *listening skills* and attention. The latter has more to do with being able to focus the mental effort, whereas listening involves being able to interpret what is being heard. Some children with difficulties in the area of communication need time, both to process what they hear and time to form their thoughts in order to make a response. As teachers are keen to maintain the momentum and pace of lessons, it is not always easy to give pupils the time they may need, but it is important to try to differentiate between pupils who do not understand what they have been told and those who need time to explain what they know.

As well as being able to listen to what others are saying, it is important to be able to understand the emotions they are expressing. Usually people learn to do this without being taught. They learn to see different *emotions* on people's faces and to express such emotions themselves; they learn to differentiate between the tone of a voice used in anger and to contrast it with a friendly tone; and they observe from a person's posture and the gestures they use, how they are feeling. People who cannot recognise emotions in others rarely express the subtleties of emotion themselves. They may scream with unhappiness and throw a tantrum when cross or upset, but their voice will be flat at other times and their faces will lack expression. It is not easy to acquire the ability to read others' emotions or to express one's own emotions in an acceptable and less extreme manner, if a natural understanding is not there. However, even if it may never come naturally, children can be helped to understand emotion in others and to regulate their own behaviour.

There was a time when teachers did most of the *talking* rather than their pupils. Nowadays, there is likely to be a better balance, but it is still important to make sure pupils have the opportunity to share ideas with peers, to discuss their ideas in groups of different sizes and to have the opportunity of talking in front of the class or school. Some will relish these opportunities, others will need to grow in confidence before they are ready to speak in front of an audience of any size. A solid foundation in listening and speaking are prerequisites for learning to read and write, yet less emphasis has been placed on these vital skills as foundations for literacy. Furthermore, it is through exchanging ideas, through having discussions and taking part in debates that thinking develops. Children with SLI may miss out on some of these activities unless care is taken to make sure they are able to participate in a way they find manageable.

Figure 4.6   Strategies for communication skills

- Develop pupils' ability to listen by gradually increasing the length of time they are expected to do so.

- Encourage pupils to listen carefully to each other and to a range of other people talking to different sized groups.

- Provide opportunities for discussion in pairs and in different sized groups.

- Use radio programmes and other forms of listening where pupils can learn to concentrate on one medium without other distractions.

- Use games to develop listening and attention skills, such as identifying taped sounds.

- Use percussion instruments for children to create rhythms and to practise following instructions to play and to stop playing.

- Break instructions into chunks and check understanding by asking pupils to repeat back what it is they have to do.

- Make more use of signs, symbols, pictures and photographs as teaching aids.

- Revise key concepts and vocabulary regularly.

- Teach vocabulary specific to each subject and have it on display or inside the books of pupils who need it.

- Practise oral skills in pairs, groups and in front of the class.

- Use specific games to help with the development of social communication skills: ICT programmes on recognising emotion, guessing what emotions pupils are demonstrating by facial expressions, or role playing different emotions.

- Give pupils the opportunity to record their own voices and to hear themselves speaking.

- Include debating sessions in lessons and encourage all pupils to make a contribution, however short.

 Photocopiable:

Literacy

In the normal order of events, infants develop speech through listening to those around them talking. Having acquired speech, they will later be able to master reading, which involves getting meaning from the printed page. Having interpreted what others have written (for example, recognising their name), they are in a position to learn to write themselves. However, it was mentioned earlier that reading and writing, unlike listening and speaking, are not natural activities, and children will vary in the point at which they are developmentally ready to start becoming literate. There is a need to distinguish between pupils who are simply not ready for formal teaching, but who need to be immersed in the joy of picture books and the excitement of sharing stories so that they will be motivated to learn to read and develop an understanding of what it means to be a reader, and those who need very specific teaching because of a condition such as dyslexia.

The multisensory approach to encouraging children with significant *reading* difficulties is the one that works best, because it allows children to use their strengths, while working on areas of weakness. Reading combines integrating auditory information (about the sounds of which words are composed) and visual information (about the shape and appearance of letters and whole words). Pupils need a whole range of strategies to support their reading, including sounding out words, building up a sight vocabularly and knowing how to use the context, including any graphic information.

While *spelling* is the other main area of difficulty for those with dyslexia, those with dysgraphia or dyspraxia will have trouble with the actual production of handwriting. As this is to do with movement, it is covered under the strategies for motor skills. Turning to spelling, pupils with a good visual memory will manage the irregularities of English spelling, because they will remember when a word looks right. For others without this ability, learning to spell in a language where there are nearly as many exceptions as words that follow the rule can be hard work. A multisensory approach would seem beneficial here as well.

Numeracy

Far less attention has been paid to becoming numerate compared to the emphasis placed on learning to read and write. It is comparatively recently, for instance, that dyscalculia has started to be recognised as another type of specific learning difficulty. Whereas dyslexia has been described as a dysfunction in the reception, comprehension, or production of linguistic information, dyscalculia has been described as a dysfunction in the reception, comprehension, or production of quantitative and spatial information. As well as lacking the intuitive number sense that most people possess, those who struggle to become numerate may have difficulty:

- understanding simple number concepts such as counting

- learning number facts

- understanding size and the relative magnitude of numbers

- carrying out the procedures to do with number.

In addition, they may have problems with shape and space, handling money and learning the concepts of direction, sequencing and time.

Figure 4.7 Strategies for literacy skills

- Try to identify those with dyslexia and those who are slow to make a start at reading.

- Help pupils to understand that words are made up of sounds by developing phonological awareness through a multisensory approach.

- Provide additional opportunities for practice if blending sounds into words is problematic. Make them interactive.

- Utilise pupils' visual strengths if they cannot learn through a phonic approach by encouraging them to build up a sight vocabulary, starting with their own name and the names of others in the class.

- Encourage pupils to enjoy books and to learn about what is involved in reading, even if they are not ready to learn to read until they are six or seven.

- Ensure pupils develop a range of strategies, including making use of the context by reading beyond the word they do not know and using any graphic clues.

- Make sure struggling readers engage in reading more often rather than less frequently, but with support.

- Help pupils with hyperlexia to develop the ability to understand what they read by reducing the complexity of the material and asking them questions about it.

- Use talking books and ones where pupils can record their own voices to increase their motivation.

- Recognise that some pupils may not be ready to learn spelling rules before seven years of age or older.

- Take a multisensory approach to spelling and handwriting as well as to reading.

- Ensure pupils who need it have daily practice in handwriting, while not being asked to think about anything apart from the formation of the letters.

- Allow opportunities to tell or record stories, rather than always being expected to write them out.

- Use alternative methods of recording as well: mind maps, diagrams, charts, writing frames, digital cameras, etc.

 Photocopiable:

Educating Children with Complex Conditions © Winand H. Dittrich and Rona Tutt, 2008.

For any pupils experiencing difficulties, whether they are dyscalculic or not, it is important that no gaps are left, but that learners have a thorough understanding of one stage before moving on to the next. This is because numerical learning is hierarchical. When a pupil is unable to make progress, it is necessary to go back to the point at which their understanding fails, however far back that is. For those lacking an intuitive sense of number, as well as those whose understanding is insecure, it is important to put mathematical concepts into a real life context: using opportunities to count objects in the environment, handling real money to make transactions, using the classroom clock or pupils' watches to keep track of the time, and drawing attention to diaries and calendars. In this way, not only will pupils see numbers as part of their lives and learn to be more comfortable with them, but they will have additional visual and tactile information to support their understanding.

Socialisation

Learning at school is mainly a social experience. In his recent book, *Mental Health in Schools,* Mark Prever talks of secondary schools, in particular, being like 'cauldrons of emotions' where:

> thoughts, feelings and behaviours ricochet like a pinball machine, forming almost infinite permutations. (2006: 70)

The majority of children are naturally gregarious and thrive on the company of others, despite the ups and downs of various friendships. For some children with developmental disorders, relationships will be more problematic, either because they do not understand people: how they think and feel, or even that they *do* think and feel, or because they do not understand the give and take of friendship. School is an opportunity to learn to relate to different age groups, to cope with different size groupings and with different settings.

Schools are now being encouraged to take a greater interest in their pupils' social and emotional well being. **Emotional intelligence**, **emotional literacy** and **circle time** are now part of educational language. This works well for the majority of children, but a few will need additional support in understanding how to make allowances for the needs of others as well as their own needs.

It is never going to be easy to teach social skills to those who do not pick them up naturally by mixing with others. Solutions need to be found to help them acquire these skills, regardless of whether it is because they lack self-awareness and an awareness of other people's needs, or they have difficulty in conforming to school rules and expectations. Once again, the first step is to accept that specific teaching is required, whether it is modelling **pretend play**, learning about **turn-taking**, or targeting unwanted behaviours. Children may not accommodate the needs of others because they do not recognise them or because they find it hard to control their own impulses. So the next step is find out why they behave in a way that is interfering with their ability to make friends and to decide what aspect of their behaviour it is most important to concentrate on first. No child is going to change overnight and so there is a need to prioritise the behaviours that need to be established, whether this is helping the child with ASD to understand how their actions impinge on others, or supporting the pupil with ADHD develop ways of pausing to think before acting. It

Figure 4.8 Strategies for numeracy skills

- Use real objects for counting in sequence and for establishing the concept of what numbers stand for.

- Do exercises and activities involving right and left.

- Reinforce position words by getting pupils to move physically in response to hearing the word.

- Provide practical apparatus, including an abacus for understanding place value. Let pupils continue to have this support for as long as they need it.

- Make sure pupils are counting on, not going back to the beginning each time.

- Draw attention to number patterns and numbers in the classroom: calendars, clocks, watches, etc.

- Use real money and clock faces where pupils can move the hands.

- Encourage estimation and then checking the answers: how many paper clips or pencils are there? How wide is the desk? How many paces from their desk to the door?

- Practise estimating 10 seconds, 30 seconds, 1 minute, etc. until pupils have acquired a sense of time.

- Encourage pupils to discuss mathematical terms, have them on display, or put them inside the exercise books of pupils who need them.

- Play games finding the quickest way to guess a number.

- Use board games involving dice, or a pack of playing cards, so that numbers are used in different contexts.

- Make use of maths computer programs that provide very visual representations of the four rules of number, as well as other areas such as fractions.

- Pair pupils together with a more advanced pupil assisting the other one to play a computer or card game.

- Involve pupils who need to gain confidence in becoming familiar with numbers to keep the score in class quizzes and ball games.

- Ask pupils to explain what they are doing to check understanding and to help them to remember procedures.

Figure 4.9   Strategies for social skills

- Provide opportunities for working one-to-one with an adult and then with a partner.

- Pair pupils with those who are good role models for some classroom activities, or to give them someone to talk to at playtimes.

- Involve pupils in activities that require turn-taking and pretend play.

- Work up to pupils being able to cooperate in small groups for some activities.

- Use circle time to encourage social interaction and communication and to ensure that everyone learns to take turns and to join in.

- Give pupils collaborative learning tasks without forcing any pupil to participate who is not yet at that stage.

- Make sure pupils do not become too dependent on adults but learn independence skills.

- Use social stories to explain to pupils how to behave in different situations. These can be in written or picture form.

- Try to make sure that pupils are praised for behaving well rather than getting attention when they are not. Positive reinforcement works better than punishment.

- Give low-key prompts about desired behaviour, such as quietly dropping a picture on the desk showing the desired behaviour.

- Talk to them on their own rather than in front of the class when they need to be reminded of school and class rules.

- Go over class rules regularly with pupils and get them to contribute their ideas as to what they should be.

- Make it clear what the expectations are of how pupils will behave and help them to live up to them by having a positive approach.

- Use puppet plays, role play and drama devised by the pupils which explore people's feelings and attitudes to events.

- Model social skills by maintaining good relationships with pupils and giving a high priority to their social development.

- Look beyond the child who is frightened by their lack of control or miserable with how they are.

Photocopiable:

can be overwhelming both for the pupils concerned and for the staff to think how much there is to be done in order to see a marked improvement in social skills, but by planning one step at a time and agreeing what that step should be, small steps towards eventual progress can be identified.

🔑 Key points Learning and the brain

- The brain develops through mental activity of all kinds.

- Learners need to know that about the brain's plasticity and have confidence in their ability to succeed.

- Learning occurs when the learner is motivated and actively engaged.

- As learning is an accumulative process based on neurological development, new learning needs to build on previous knowledge.

- Learning will be retained if it is understood and practised. Those who find learning difficult may need more practice than those who learn easily.

- Short bursts of physical activity and times for recreation enhance learning.

- Both teachers and those who are taught need to adopt a range of styles.

- Pupils' interest will be captured by the unexpected, so teachers need to ensure that their lessons have an element of surprise about them.

🗔 Summary

This chapter has concentrated on moving beyond the labels pupils are given to look at ways of helping them to make progress.

Knowing how the brain learns has been emphasised as important in knowing how best to help pupils who are experiencing difficulties.

The importance of taking a multisensory approach to teaching and providing opportunities for pupils to learn and respond in different ways has been stressed.

Common areas of difficulties that go across some of the neurodevelopmental disorders have been discussed.

Strategies have been suggested which can help children to overcome areas of difficulty.

Further Reading 📖

Kirby, A. (2006) *Mapping SEN*. London: David Fulton.

O'Brien, J. (1996) *Lightning Learning*. Chichester: The Quantum Group.

Reid, G. (2007) *Motivating Learners in the Classroom*. London: Paul Chapman Publishing.

Sousa, D.A. (2001) *How the Special Needs Brain Learns*. Thousands Oaks, CA: Corwin Press.

5

Environmental issues and therapeutic approaches

> **This chapter covers:**
>
> - the part the environment plays in neurodevelopmental disorders
> - whether diet is a significant factor in these conditions
> - whether the use of supplements can play a part in contributing to a child's well-being
> - whether the use of medication can be justified in helping children (and the adults around them) to cope with their difficulties
> - the need for psychological support in schools
> - which therapies and therapists may need to be part of the support offered to pupils with developmental disorders.

Adverse factors in the environment

How children's brains develop will depend not just on how far normal development is able to take place and whether there are genetic or neurological abnormalities, but also on the environment, both in the womb and after birth. Unfortunately, maximum impact can occur during the early months of pregnancy, when the mother may not even be aware that she is carrying a child. This means that she may not be particularly concerned about environmental hazards, such as the lack of a nutritional diet, the effects of minor diseases such as influenza, or the impact of any drugs she may be taking. While the effects of smoking and drinking are recognised, and the dangers of drugs like thalidomide are well established, the physical damage that may be caused by other environmental factors is not yet fully understood. Examples of how brain development may be affected include:

- tobacco, alcohol and drug abuse, all of which can cause damage during pregnancy to the developing infant

- the umbilical cord being twisted, so that it temporarily cuts off the supply of oxygen to the brain, damaging neurons and leading to learning disorders

- stress in the child's environment leading to **corticosteroids** being released into the bloodstream, damaging the hippocampus and interfering with memory

73

- dioxins and other toxins during pregnancy, or at an early age, disrupting brain cell growth and development (for example, lead in paint and water pipes), resulting in poisoning, brain disorders and learning difficulties)

- neglect, violent behaviour and traumatic events which can have adverse effects on the learning of children.

On the whole, infants will develop normally and it is not helpful to be over anxious about all the possibilities that may have an adverse affect. But there are growing concerns that an increasingly unnatural environment may be putting susceptible children at risk. Being aware of these risks well in advance can help prospective parents to take a sensible look at how some of these factors might be reduced. As has been shown, the genetic make up which might lead to subtle brain dysfunctions, can result in one of a number of related disorders, rather than the direct inheritance of specific abilities or disabilities. While little can be done to influence the genes, the combination of the genetic component with other factors is what is thought to lead to neurodevelopmental disorders. As more is discovered about what might be damaging in the environment, both before and after birth, the possibility increases that some risk factors may be avoidable.

However, this is not going to be an easy matter to resolve, as, with the onward march of technology, new factors keep entering the equation. Today's landscape is littered with phone masts (many disguised) in addition to pylons. An increasing number of younger children have their own mobile phones, raising concerns about the amount of time some spend with a phone held close to their still developing brains, while in schools there are similar queries about the proliferation of electromagnetic waves from wi-fi systems (wireless computer networks) as well. There is much to be discovered about what is and is not safe and, unfortunately, the scenario is likely to become more and more complex. Knowledge about the adverse effects of new inventions and public debates about their safety, often lag well behind the use of new technologies.

〰 Questions for reflection

1   Of the elements in the environment mentioned above, which cause you concern? Do you think there is any evidence that you should be concerned?

2   Are there any factors not listed here that you feel might be a danger to children's physical or mental health?

3   Can you think of anything that might be done to ensure the invention of new technologies is matched by a consideration of any risks?

Diet, nutrition and the role of supplements

Turning to diet, a similar picture emerges, in that huge advances have been made in providing an ever wider range of foods from across the globe. This would seem to be most welcome. However, changes in food production and in retailing, as well as in the way people choose to eat their food has resulted in more natural foods being replaced by ready-made meals that are full of preservatives, additives and E-numbers.

A number of celebrity chefs have made a name for themselves and people enjoy watching them prepare meals on television programmes, yet cooking is actually in danger of becoming a spectator sport in many families. Sitting down regularly together to enjoy home-cooked meals has been replaced in many households by chilled, frozen and microwavable meals, or trips to a burgeoning number of restaurants and takeaways. An exotic array of food from different countries and the availability all year round of many fresh vegetables and fruits provide more raw ingredients than ever before. However, a combination of frenetic lifestyles and the marketing of ready-made meals, mean that people are less likely to spend time on food preparation. A habit of snacking has crept in and constant snacking is less likely to provide the necessary nutrients to grow and maintain healthy bodies than meals eaten with a knife and fork.

In order to preserve food for longer, to make it colourful and attractive to the eye and seductive to the taste buds, a bewildering array of E-numbers and other additives are to be found in many of the foods on supermarket shelves. Organic foods are increasingly being sought as finding food in something like its natural state is becoming more difficult. Although the content of what is in tins and packets of food has to be displayed, it needs a magnifying glass in one hand and a dictionary in the other to understand the intricacies of the information. How many people, for instance, manage to differentiate between fruit-flavoured desserts (meaning that they have a little fruit in them) and those that are described as fruit-flavour desserts (where the taste will not be derived from the actual fruit, but from an artificial substitute)?

While a healthy, nutritious diet is recognised as being important, particularly for children and young people who are still growing, too much of the wrong food or too little of the right food may have a particularly adverse effect on some individuals prone to neurodevelopmental disorders. There is growing evidence that too much sugar, salt and certain colourings can make children hyperactive and less able to concentrate. It is not hard to imagine how this effect will be magnified in children who have ADHD. While a bad diet alone is unlikely to cause ADHD, it is clear that it can exacerbate the condition. Some children with ADHD have a much stronger reaction to certain substances in their diet than others, but all are likely to benefit from a better balanced, more natural diet.

There has been a great deal of controversy about the effects of certain foods on children with ASD, with many parents testifying to the difference made by putting their children on a gluten-free/casein-free diet (the GF/CF diet). Luke Jackson, a teenager with ASD, felt so strongly about the beneficial effects of changing the diet of himself and his brothers that he wrote a book about it when he was twelve (see Further Reading at the end of this chapter). Between them, Luke and two of his brothers had diagnoses of ADHD and ASD. Whereas those who have coeliac disease need to follow a strict gluten-free diet, there is evidence that some children with ASD (and to a lesser extent ADHD) are better on a GF/CF diet, which seems to ease their bowel problems as well as other symptoms affecting their well-being. This diet is not an easy one to follow as gluten is found in most grains (cutting out everything made from normal flour) and casein in dairy products (cutting out milk, butter and cheese). However, many parents will testify to the very real difference following these or similar diets have made to their children's well-being.

Millions are pumped into schemes trying to do something about children's behaviour in and out of school, yet very little is spent on researching the adverse effects of a diet low in nutrients and high in artificial substances. The rise in the number of schools running 'breakfast clubs' is due in part to concerns about children arriving at school, either with an inadequate breakfast inside them or none at all. Teachers see the listlessness of the child who has had no breakfast, the hyperactivity of the child whose lunch has consisted of a sugary fizzy drink, a packet of crisps laden with monosodium glutamate and a couple of bars of chocolate, and the inability to concentrate of the child who is inadequately nourished. Where money is spent on researching diet, it is more likely to be used for looking at the physical effects, for instance concerns about childhood obesity, than on the links between diet and a child's mental health and behaviour.

While a good diet should be able to provide all the necessary nutrients for a healthy body and mind, in effect it is quite difficult to make sure any diet is fully nutritious. Supplements are being suggested by some as being necessary in a way that they were not in the past. While this is another controversial area, it is one that needs further consideration in order to add to the sum of knowledge about how to ensure that children have the best possible start in life. As well as multivitamins and minerals, there has been a growing interest in the use of essential fat supplements, especially omega-3, which is being seen as a possible way of improving children's attention and decreasing their anxiety and aggression. It has taken time to realise that developed countries can still have malnourished children and that the growing incidence of childhood obesity is a sign of being overfed without necessarily being well nourished, but when it is debated publicly that some of today's children are in danger of having a shorter life expectancy than their parents, it is time to take a serious look at what is happening to children's diet.

〰️ Questions for reflection

1   What more might be done to encourage people who take an interest in programmes about cooking to put what they see into practice?

2   Are you aware of any children who have been put on a special diet and did you notice any beneficial and/or adverse effects?

3   Do you think there is a role for children taking supplements and, if so, do you think that there is any evidence that they may be particularly helpful in cases where children have neurodevelopmental disorders?

The use of medication

The idea of having to turn to medication to help with children's learning and behavioural difficulties is bound to be an emotive subject. In the case of neurodevelopmental disorders, the question arises mainly in relation to ADHD and ASD, with people being divided about whether or not medication should be used.

In the case of ADHD, which is seen partly as an abnormality in brain chemistry creating an imbalance in certain neurotransmitters, most likely dopamine and serotonin, it has been argued that it makes sense to use a biochemical remedy, such as amphetamine-based drugs, which are stimulants. Although Ritalin®, the best known of these drugs, is much more widely used in America, it is also becoming increasingly common in this country to prescribe it for ADHD. In 1993, there were 3,500 children on Ritalin®; by 2006, this had risen to 250, 000. The idea is that this type of medication helps to decrease hyperactivity and impulsivity, enabling children to focus better on their work. There can be immediate side effects and some children experience a loss of appetite, mood swings or interference with their sleep patterns.

A longer-term concern is that drug dependency can be habit forming; the person becomes addicted to the experience of taking tablets and feels unable to cope with life without them. Ritalin®, for instance, is chemically similar to speed or cocaine. Obviously there are concerns about putting children on medication for any length of time and many people will want to explore other avenues first, including helping parents to understand and cope with their child's behaviour, using psychological therapies, or trying out the effects of any dietary changes, including the possibility of using supplements.

Adjustments made in these areas may reduce the need for medication except in a minority of cases, where the child is unable to learn because of the intensity of their symptoms. If a drug is prescribed, it may give schools an opportunity to develop their pupil's work habits. However, it should not be seen as solving the problem, but used in combination with other approaches. Children with the other neurodevelopmental disorders are less likely to be on drugs, although it is not uncommon for those on the autistic spectrum to be put on medication to deal with difficult periods of their lives, including during adolescence.

 Questions for reflection

1   Do you have any pupils who are on medication for ADHD or ASD and, if so, do you think this is a sensible way to help them overcome their difficulties?

2   What is the child's attitude to taking medication?

3   What is your school's approach to helping pupils to understand that the difference between taking drugs prescribed by a doctor and taking 'recreational' drugs?

The role of psychologists, therapists and therapies

Therapists are healthcare professionals rather than being part of the education service. This can cause friction between the education and health services. Although education and social care have moved closer together under the Children Act of 2004, with combined structures for delivering services to children, young people and their families, the links with the health service have been harder to put in place, as they often have different systems and areas that are not coterminus with a local authority. Yet, for children with SEN, therapists can play a vital role in addressing their needs.

Most schools are able to call on the services of an attached educational psychologist (EP), but there is seldom enough time for them to see all the pupils who would benefit from being assessed, let alone time to work one-to-one with pupils, or even to be able to advise staff on the management of pupils with complex conditions. Any contact with clinical psychologists or neuropsychologists is minimal.

Of the many different types of therapy and therapists that exist, the role of speech and language specialists (SaLTs) is the most significant in terms of the numbers of pupils who need their support. For programmes to work best, the SaLT needs to work closely with both school staff and with the family. This has become more possible as SaLTs have moved out of clinics and into school settings. A further move has been to work in the classroom rather than seeing pupils on their own elsewhere on the school premises. This provides better opportunities for pupils to generalise the skills they are learning, as well as making it easier for therapists and school staff to work more closely together. To ease a shortage, some teaching assistants are developing their skills under the guidance of SaLTs, so that they can take a lead in making sure programmes are carried through. Some of these may be trained sufficiently to become SaLT Assistants.

Clearly, children with specific language impairments (SLI), and autistic spectrum disorders (ASD) require the expertise of specialists who are experts in the field of speech and language development and disorders. Because of the close links between some of the specific learning difficulties (SpLD) and language development, they may have an input here as well. Although difficulties in this area are not one of the symptoms of ADHD, as 30–35 percent of those with the diagnosis have additional speech and language disorders, they will also need the services of SaLTs. This shows up the high level of need for qualified SaLTs and there are never enough of them to go round. This causes serious problems, as speech is an area that needs to be tackled while children are still young enough to respond. As they grow older, young people will become increasingly self-conscious about their failure to understand or use speech effectively and any wrong habits will be harder to eradicate. The government is aware of the need for more and better training and in 2007 took some positive steps to improve the situation. These are discussed further in the final chapter.

Less common in schools, but highly valued where they are present, are physiotherapists (physios) and occupational therapists (OTs). Physios work mainly on helping children with coordinating their gross motor skills and improving their balance, while OTs specialise in the development of fine motor skills. Sometimes physios and OTs work alongside each other, as often they will be working with the same children. Some OTs are beginning to specialise in helping children, including those with ASD who have sensory integration problems.

As the extent of the overlap and co-existence of developmental disorders begins to unfold, it becomes clear that there should be a greater emphasis on the importance of motor skills. Physios and OTs may need to be as common in schools as SaLTs need to be. In a recent survey of 50 children with a diagnosis of dyspraxia undertaken by the Dyscovery Centre at the University of Wales, only 14 percent had dyspraxia as a single disorder, while the rest either had dyslexia, ADHD or ASD, or they had the following combinations of difficulties:

- dyspraxia plus dyslexia and ASD

- dyspraxia plus ADHD and ASD

- dyspraxia plus dyslexia plus ADHD and ASD

- dyspraxia plus ADHD plus ASD and SLI

- dyspraxia plus dyslexia plus ASD and SLI

- dyspraxia plus dyslexia plus ADHD plus ASD and SLI.

While it is not clear whether there was no evidence of dyscalculia or dysgraphia being present or whether these were not assessed, it is interesting to note that all four of the disorders that have been the focus of this book are mentioned here in connection with each other.

Some schools and clinics are fortunate enough to have one or more of the less traditional therapies, such as art, music, drama or play therapy. Therapists working in this way provide children and young people with a means of communication that does not rely on language. This gives them a chance to explore their feelings in a non-directive way, which the therapist is then able to interpret. These approaches can be particularly beneficial for individuals who either cannot, or who are reluctant to, communicate through language.

∿ Questions for reflection

1   What therapists do you have in your school and have they altered the way they work?

2   Do school staff and therapists have a chance to talk about the children they share on a regular basis?

3   What therapists would you like to see working in your school and what contribution do you think they would be able to make?

Putting it all together

In her book, *Toxic Childhood*, Sue Palmer discusses the rise in the diagnosis of developmental disorders including ADHD, ASD and what she terms the 'dyslexia cluster' of dyslexia, dysgraphia, dyscalculia and dyspraxia, as well as a general concern that more children without labels are having problems in concentrating, exercising self-restraint and taking account of other people's needs and interests. The term 'toxic childhood' expresses her view that a whole galaxy of technological and cultural changes may be having an adverse effect on young children's development. She writes:

> The more I found out, the clearer it became that trying to tackle any one of these elements independently of the others was a waste of time – they all swirl together in a toxic mix. So just improving children's diet, for instance, isn't enough – all sorts of other things impinge on it: TV and marketing messages, exercise and sleeping habits, childcare arrangements, parenting style. (2006: 15)

There are many signs of a growing concern about how current lifestyles are having an adverse effect on children's upbringing and development. While many children are resilient and seem to take in their stride family break-up or the lack of an extended family nearby, the more vulnerable or fragile may not have the skills or the confidence to deal with the uncertainties life throws at them, or to cope with a constantly changing world.

It is obvious that children who are well nourished will feel more able to learn and to enjoy life. While diet cannot cure complex conditions, it can make a contribution to pupils' ability to succeed. Diet needs to be seen as one of the factors that give children a better chance of making the most of their potential. It is accepted that bodies cannot grow without the proper food, but less has been said about the fuel needed by the brain if it is to function well. All children need to be well nourished, but for children who start at a disadvantage because of a neurological abnormality, it should be seen as even more important, indeed as part of a holistic approach to helping them, to do everything possible to assist them in becoming effective learners. Whether or not that includes some form of medication for a period of their lives is for the medical profession, together with their families, to decide. The option should be considered, but, preferably, only after other changes and approaches (for example, some form of **cognitive behavioural therapy**) have been tried first.

Astonishingly, it was not until the lack of nutrients in many school dinners had been exposed by Jamie Oliver in his television series that the drive was on to improve pupils' diet. By then, some schools no longer had kitchens or cooks who had been trained to do more than open packets of pre-prepared food. While some school cooks and their staff had been working miracles in turning out appetising meals on a shoestring, others needed to be trained or re-trained. Meanwhile, schools have had to make the switch from relying on vending machines to supplement the school budget to offering healthy snacks and drinks, and, harder still, persuading pupils to accept them. However, help is at hand. Cookery lessons where pupils make real meals is to replace food technology and the significance of a balanced diet for growing children is at last being recognised.

Finally, the role of additional professional support staff, including therapists with different specialisms, needs to be recognised, in order to meet the needs of pupils with a range of difficulties, including those with complex conditions. Not only are far more needed in schools, but the move towards integrating their work with the rest of the school's activities is vital. So much more can be done if teachers, support staff, psychologists and therapists share their skills and their knowledge about children with learning difficulties and the ways in which they can be helped to become successful learners.

Summary

This chapter has considered the need to take a more holistic view of children's needs.

It has been suggested that the effects of environmental factors on the brain should be taken into account, as well as the role played by giving the brain the food it needs to enable children to learn effectively.

It has been suggested that medication should not be seen as a solution in its own right, but that if it is used, it should always be in combination with other changes and approaches being tried.

Finally, the point has been made that school staff, parents and other professionals should work closely together, in order that information, knowledge and skills are shared.

Further Reading

Holford, P. and Colson, D. (2006) *Optimum Nutrition for Your Child's Mind*. London: Piaktus Books.

Jackson, L. (2002) *A User Guide to the GF/CF Diet for Autism, Asperger's Syndrome and AD/HD*. London: Jessica Kingsley.

Lathe, R. (2006) *Autism, Brain and Environment*. London: Jessica Kingsley.

Palmer, S. (2006) *Toxic Childhood*. London: Orion.

6

A consideration of complex conditions

This final chapter draws together the threads that have been running through the book. In particular, it highlights:

- the outcome of the case studies of Tommy and Sylvie from Chapter 1
- the causes of the overlap and co-existence of neurodevelopmental disorders
- the need to concentrate on what pupils find hard rather than their labels
- using what is known about how the brain works when devising strategies to help them
- recent developments in education and their relevance to pupils with complex conditions
- ideas to develop a better future.

The case studies continued

The opening chapter began with two case studies. Tommy aged eight had originally been diagnosed with ADHD, a label that was later changed to ASD. Sylvie aged twelve had dyspraxia added to her diagnosis of dyslexia.

 Case study 6.1: Tommy and Sylvie

After Tommy's diagnosis was changed, the head teacher, the special educational needs coordinator (SENCo), Tommy's teacher and his parents had a meeting at which it was agreed to seek advice from the local authority's SEN support service. An advisory teacher for autism came to the school to observe Tommy and to talk to him. She confirmed that his behaviour suggested he was on the autistic spectrum, that he was hypersensitive to both noise and to touch, and that his inability to concentrate was the result of sensory overload. On her advice, Tommy was given a desk partially screened off from the rest of the class and away from a heater, whose noise had been upsetting him. His teacher

(Continued)

(Continued)

made sure she addressed him by name each time she gave instructions to the class about the next activity. A teaching assistant made sure he knew what to do before helping other pupils. When staff realised that Tommy had lashed out in response to a teacher encouraging him to return to the class by placing a hand on his shoulder, staff tried to avoid physical contact, while his parents worked with him at home to make him less sensitive. Once his difficulties were understood and some allowances made for him, Tommy settled down and began to get increasing satisfaction from his work.

Once the diagnosis of dyspraxia was made, it was agreed that the teaching assistant (TA), who delivered Sylvie's daily reading and spelling programme, would work with the head of the PE department and the physiotherapist, who had made the diagnosis, to develop Sylvie's coordination and balance. The SENCo took the opportunity to include other pupils with dyspraxia, who had a 10-minute programme of motor skills every morning. In collaboration with the occupational therapist, it was agreed that Sylvie would be given a laptop and taught touch-typing in an after school club. This took the pressure off her trying to write legibly. The OT also gave her a series of exercises to train muscle coordination in fine motor tasks and pre-writing exercises to strengthen the muscles involved in fine motor skills, which she practised every day at home for 10 minutes. After several months, her writing started to become legible and this increased her self-esteem considerably.

Although it may not always be possible to give pupils all the help they need or to have access to the professional advice that is needed, some adjustments to the pupil's curriculum and environment can make a real difference. Once Tommy's difficulties were better understood, it was possible to avoid situations that had caused him to lose control and become violent. When Sylvie was given support for her co-existing conditions, her motivation returned and her work began to improve.

This book has explored some of the links between the diagnostic labels that are used, what is going on in the brain and the effect this may have on pupils' learning. From this, certain strands have emerged which will be considered next.

Synthesising the strands

Given that there is still so much to be discovered about the workings of the brain and the relationship with learning and behaviour, any conclusions can only be tentative. A more scientific approach to learning has only just begun. However, certain strands are beginning to emerge about how complex conditions may be viewed.

Overlap and co-morbidity

There is increasing evidence of overlap and co-existence between the neurodevelopmental disorders of ADHD, ASD, SLI and the specific learning difficulties of dyslexia, dyspraxia, dyscalculia and dysgraphia. They appear to have:

- overlapping symptoms

- a tendency to co-exist with each other

- a common aetiology in terms of being likely to result from a combination of neurological and other factors.

Indeed, it would appear that neurodevelopmental disorders do not stem from the direct inheritance of specific abilities and disabilities, but from a neurological abnormality resulting in one of a number of related disorders. This could explain why members of the same family have different conditions. For instance, the seven children in the Jackson family (who were the inspiration for the BBC television drama *Magnificent 7*), consist of three girls who have no disorders, and four boys, who between them have ADHD, ASD including Asperger's syndrome, dyslexia and dyspraxia. There is some emerging evidence that this overlap and co-morbidity corresponds with what is known to date about the parts of the brain that are affected in the different disorders that have been discussed.

Aetiology and education

Although it is clear that there are no single genes that cause these conditions, an abnormality in the early development of the brain, either as a result of genetic factors, or from damage to the brain cells and their connections, would appear to predispose some infants to developing these conditions. However, what happens next depends on other factors that act as triggers. While the exact nature of these triggers has yet to be discovered, it is possible, for instance, that toxins in the environment both before and after birth, the lack of proper nutrition, the effects of illness, and other factors yet to be recognised, may all play a part. What is becoming clear is that the brain's plasticity, and its ability to grow and adapt throughout life, means that there is always hope of improvement. Children in particular are able to increase their understanding, their knowledge and their skills despite the disorders they may have.

Teachers need to understand more about how the brain learns in order to inform the way they teach. This is particularly important for teaching pupils with complex conditions, as they need additional guidance in finding ways to utilise their potential. As Blakemore and Frith point out:

> It may be possible to ignore the brain when talking about normal child development, but the brain cannot be ignored when discussing developmental disorders. (2005: 6)

If teachers have this understanding, they can help pupils to develop a knowledge about how learning takes place. This should help both teachers and those who are taught to be optimistic about the possibilities, particularly as it is well known that the brain has plenty of spare capacity and an immense potential for plasticity.

From labels to symptoms

It has become clear that the diagnostic labels children receive stem in part from the training, expertise and experience of those who are making the diagnosis. The situation has become more complicated by an increasing number of children receiving more than one label. As well as accepting the need to accommodate a variety of learning styles, this may be lead to redefining what is normal and abnormal, together with what is acceptable and unacceptable behaviour. There is a need, not only to have a multi-professional assessment of single disorders, but to have places where specialists in different fields can take a holistic view of the child and the full range of difficulties he or she may have. Such places are beginning to appear, but they are few and far between.

At the present time, labels are needed to guide parents and professionals. They act as a starting point for deciding what type of support children need and how it should be delivered. However, it may be that there is a surfeit of labelling, as children with very mild symptoms, stemming from factors other than neurological abnormalities, are being labelled as well. Improved guidelines both for diagnosing neurodevelopmental disorders and for outlining therapeutic approaches that can be taken are urgently needed.

From symptoms to strategies

As the number of recognised conditions increases leading to a greater overlap between them, and as the number of pupils with more than one diagnosis becomes less exceptional, one sensible way forward is to concentrate on common areas of difficulty, rather than on labels. As described previously, psychological problems that interfere with essential learning go across the different conditions and are the direct result of brain systems that are dysfunctional.

Maintaining motivation and self-esteem are seen as key to improving pupils' learning. Knowing that intelligence is neither fixed nor one-dimensional should make it easier for pupils to think positively about their ability to learn. The brain's plasticity and its ability to develop more connections the more it is exercised should give hope to all those who are working with pupils who have SEN as well as to the individuals themselves. Added to this is the need to experience success rather than failure in order to become confident learners.

The direct teaching of skills that are usually acquired naturally needs to be recognised, whether this is teaching a child how to play, helping pupils to recognise emotion in others, or starting from scratch with pupils who have no intuitive understanding of number. The foundations for further learning must then be in place before the introduction of the next step. Any new learning should be linked to something the child already understands, so connections are made between topics and between subjects.

At all stages, pupils with developmental disorders are likely to need a greater degree of guidance and support. They need time to process and assimilate new concepts, time to rehearse new skills and time to consolidate new learning. It is not easy to give them the time that they need, but if work is covered too superficially, it will not be remembered. All too often, pupils who are slower to grasp new concepts, or those working with them, give up in despair because they seem unable to take on board new learning, yet, given more time, they might have shown that a new skill could be mastered.

Multisensory teaching will suit all pupils as well as being of particular benefit to pupils with neurodevelopmental disorders. It introduces variety into lessons as well as making it easier for pupils to learn in ways that suit them. Having a flexible approach to the needs of individuals makes it easier to create an environment in which they can succeed, whether it is allowing pupils to move around more while they work, to listen from a distance, to fiddle with concentrators or to earn certain rewards. Knowing how to create the conditions to make it easier for each child to respond is much harder in secondary schools, where subject teachers may see more than a hundred students a week. This is less of a problem where support staff are present who know the pupils well, but there still needs to be a common understanding about the degree of flexibility that exists for responding to individual needs.

Changing expectations of schools and pupils

Schools are under relentless pressure to raise standards, to implement a never-ending stream of initiatives and their associated policies, as well as extending their role to encompass the learning of families and local communities. This is the context in which school leaders and the rest of the school team have to find ways of educating pupils with increasingly complex needs. If the pressure of using simplistic 'league tables' to measure the intricacies of schools were removed, all teachers and pupils would benefit from a broader and more enjoyable curriculum, not least children with complex conditions. It is hardly surprising if, under the current regime of piling the pressure on schools, there are not enough hours in the day for school leaders and their teams to learn about the latest brain research, to understand what it means to have overlapping or co-existing disorders, or to put the two together in order to devise a more appropriate and flexible curriculum. Although there will always be the difficulty of fitting it all in and having the money to make it all happen, there are at least some developments that are encouraging and forward-looking.

The Inclusion Development Programme (IDP)

The IDP was announced in the SEN strategy *Removing Barriers to Achievement*. It was due to be launched in the autumn of 2004, but the launch finally took place in 2007. The associated material will be available to schools, those in early years education and those responsible for initial teacher training (ITT) in 2008. The IDP is a programme of professional development for school staff, focusing in 2008 on speech, language and communication needs, as well as dyslexia; then the next year on ASD, followed by BESD, including ADHD, and lastly on MLD. So far, there is no mention of dyspraxia, dyscalculia or dysgraphia, or of pupils with more complex conditions, but helping staff to understand more about the range of conditions to be found in today's classrooms is an encouraging step forward.

Also in 2007, three trusts were established:

1 the Communication Trust

2 the Dyslexia SpLD Trust

3 the Autism Education Trust.

As with the IDP, they are being run by the government in conjunction with children's charities and other organisations. The Trusts will provide access to further training, as well as providing information to enhance the understanding of those who are working with children and young people who have SEN.

The Healthy Schools Initiative

In the wake of the Jamie Oliver programmes highlighting the poor state of school food, the government established the School Food Trust. This has set out food-based standards and nutrient-based standards for food consumed on school premises, including school lunches. School cooks are being given the opportunity to receive further training, and money has been set aside to improve school kitchens.

Early in 2008, the government announced the return of cookery lessons in schools, so that all pupils have the opportunity to learn to cook simple, nutritious meals. Although it must be the parents' responsibility to provide the basis of a healthy diet, it is a step in the right direction that schools will be placing more emphasis on the importance of healthy snacks, nutritious meals and how to provide them. Hopefully, this will also create opportunities for pupils to become aware of how diet affects their physical and mental health.

Every Child Matters (ECM) and personalised learning

As has been shown, the need to treat every child as an individual is particularly important for helping those who have neurodevelopmental disorders. If the joining up of services under ECM works as intended, this should be of enormous benefit to schools, the pupils they teach, and to their families. It should lead to schools being able to draw on a much wider range of professionals. Teachers, pysychologists, therapists and others working in health and social care have a great deal to learn from each other, and the more closely they work together, the greater will be the benefit to the pupils.

Personalising learning should go beyond differentiating the curriculum to allowing greater flexibility for pupils to learn and respond in ways that make it easier for them to listen, to understand and to remain on task. It will entail not only allowing for pupils who learn and who process information at different speeds, but making allowances for those who need their own space, access to a 'time out' area, or an extra amount of physical activity during the school day. Setting individual goals based on the incremental steps of learning can help pupils to organise their efforts and be motivated to achieve, provided they meet success and not failure on the way. This is the same whether the goal is to do with changing behaviour or gaining new knowledge or skills.

A better future

Multidisciplinary research is needed to pinpoint more precisely the brain abnormalities that impede children's learning, as well as looking at the links between learning, behaviour, physical and mental health, and nutrition. This should result in a more holistic view being taken of children with complex conditions, leading to a more rounded and open-minded approach to meeting their needs. In particular, it is hoped that current interdisciplinary research into the relationship between the brain and teaching and learning will result in new teaching methods, including how to personalise and maximise the use of **e-learning** and multimedia technologies.

Multiprofessional assessment centres need to be established in all areas, so that they can be accessed by schools and families. Their role would be to work to stricter guidelines about when children should be diagnosed with developmental disorders. While this should serve to reduce the numbers being identified, it would also help to ensure that co-existing conditions were not overlooked. Children with complex conditions are better served from a neuropsychological perspective when both assessment and interventions take account of the whole environment around the child, including family situations, the school context, and any therapeutic approaches, as well as the neurological diagnosis. When a medical (and mainly deficit) model is used, any learning problems are attributed to the child without the impact of other factors being considered.

Multiagency working is essential for the proper support of children with complex conditions and a holistic view of their needs. At present, there is a danger that too many children are being prescribed drugs because of a paucity of support from across the professions. As well as more time from educational psychologists (EPs), schools should be able to access clinical psychologists to advise on therapies such as cognitive behaviour therapy (CBT) and neuropsychologists, to help bring research and education closer together and to enhance teachers' understanding of the pupils they are teaching. Closer links with CAMHS (the Child and Adolescent Mental Health Service), as well as more art, music and drama therapists working in schools would help to expand teachers' skills and give better support to pupils. In addition, speech and language therapists, physiotherapists and occupational therapists should be seen as an essential part of the school workforce rather than as a luxury or optional extra.

Joint training is needed to underpin this move. Taking people out of their separate silos and getting them to work together for the benefit of children and young people means that they must share some training. If professionals are going to respect each other's background and feel comfortable working together, then they need a common language, a mutual understanding, and even a shared set of acronyms. Clearly this will not happen overnight, but small steps are already being made, as some of the barriers between the services are being dismantled and some joint training is beginning to take place. It cannot happen soon enough for staff wrestling with how to meet pupils' diverse needs, or for the pupils themselves, who need the professionals involved with them to work together towards the same end. This common approach should involve parents and carers as well, so that schools and families are working increasingly closely together to take shared responsibility for supporting children and young people.

Multisensory teaching and learning needs to be a feature of all subjects and lessons. The need for a stimulating and encouraging environment, where there is a high level of pupil engagement and greater recognition of the need to accommodate different learning styles and behaviours, has already been stressed. Most learning depends on multisensory networks of neurons which are distributed over the whole brain. Narrowly defined learning styles (such as left/right brain learning) or single sensory teaching styles (for instance, relying too heavily on the auditory channel) are not supported by brain research. Knowledge is gained through active involvement, through the use of movement, through using the visual and auditory channels and through developing a wealth of language with which to build up concepts. Using a rich variety of activities, catching pupils' imagination and giving them the firsthand experiences to be able to link facts and events will allow even those pupils who have complex difficulties to form the memory traces needed to make a lasting impact on learning and memory.

Knowing something of how the brain works and how learning is organised in the brain leads to the following conclusions. Firstly, as children with complex conditions have difficulty in picking up and organising information for themselves, a clear, structured approach to acquiring knowledge and skills is needed. At the same time, new learning needs to be linked to previous knowledge by being embedded in a rich context of different experiences, self-initiated activities and social learning. Helping pupils' understanding by having structured teaching and having a rich learning environment are not mutually exclusive; they are complementary ways of helping all pupils to make a success of their time at school. Sometimes, pupils who have difficulties may be given a diet of repetitious exercises which run the risk of demotivating them. The challenge is to find ways of consolidating learning, while continuing to expose them to the full range of educational experiences. Neuroscience is helping to inform the search for a better quality of teaching and learning that can be adapted to the variety of conditions students may have, but neuroscience necessarily falls short of having anything to say about the wider goals and values of education and of society. Therefore, the wider social framework must form the backcloth to educational thinking.

There is always a danger that children with neurodevelopmental disorders and their families will see themselves as victims who have been given a raw deal. It is easy for the children who have difficulty in some or all areas of learning, and those who work with them in schools, to feel negative and to develop low expectations. Yet, knowledge about how the brain is constantly changing and forming new connections, and how it improves with use should help everyone concerned to remain irrepressibly optimistic about rising to the challenge of finding ways to achieve success. The brain itself has discrete areas and a mass of connections between them, which is mirrored in specific teaching of skills and concepts being linked to the richness of experience that can enthuse and inspire learners. In turning to the future, it becomes apparent that there is a need to bring the different disciplines and professions together for research, for training and for a more holistic approach to assessment. This would allow skills to be shared, leading to stronger, better coordinated support for the pupils who need it. Based on the workings of the brain, sound reasons for a multisensory approach to teaching and learning should be explored further.

The principle of balancing structured teaching of specific skills with the need for a rich and stimulating educational environment, finds its counterpart in the architecture of the brain, namely, separate areas of the brain that have incredibly rich connections. It is not the case that those who have difficulty in learning should have a narrow and impoverished diet, but that they should be given every opportunity to develop their intellectual curiosity, to acquire a love of learning and to experience the joy of taking part, as spectators and as participants, in sport, the creative arts and the positive experiences that life has to offer.

Summary

This chapter has summarised some of the themes of the book by clarifying the common features of neurodevelopmental disorders and suggesting that there should be a more multi-professional approach to assessment, to help identify co-existing disorders.

The need to know more about how the brain learns has been seen as important in supporting children with complex conditions. A more scientific approach to teaching and learning is only just beginning and there is much to be discovered about the workings of the brain.

The relevance of some of the government's initiatives has been mentioned, particularly the potential of the Inclusion Development Programme (IDP) and the associated Trusts to increase the ability of school staff to meet children's needs.

The emphasis on personalising learning should help school staff to feel confident in adapting, not just the curriculum, but their approach to each individual and his or her needs.

Useful addresses

ADDIS (Attention Deficit Disorder Information Services)
info@addis.co.uk
www.addiss.co.uk

Autism Education Trust
www.autism.org.uk

Afasic (for speech and language difficulties)
info@afasic.rog.uk
www.afasic.org.uk

BDA (The British Dyslexia Association)
info@dyslexiahelp-bda.demon.co.uk
www.bda-dyslexia.org.uk

The Communication Trust
www.thecommunicationtrust.org.uk

Dyslexia Action (formerly The Dyslexia Institute)
www.dyslexiaaction.org.uk
info@dyslexiaaction.org.uk

The Dyslexia-SpLD Trust
www.thedyslexia-spldtrust.org.uk

The Dyspraxia Foundation
dyspraxiafoundation@hotmail.com
www.dyspraxiafoundation.org.uk

ICAN (for communication difficulties)
info@ican.org.uk
www.ican.org.uk

The Inclusion Development Programme
www.standards.dcsf.gov.uk

Nasen (National Association for Special Educational Needs)
welcome@nasen.org.uk
www.nasen.org.uk

The National Austistic Society
www.nas.org.uk
nas@nas.orf.uk

Glossary

adrenaline: a hormone secreted by the adrenal glands and a central nervous system neurotransmitter released by some neurons. It is a potent stimulator of the sympathetic nervous system, increasing blood pressure, stimulating the heart muscle, accelerating the heart rate, and increasing cardiac output.

aetiology: a) the study of the causes or origins of disease or the cause; b) the origin of a disease or disorder as determined by medical diagnosis.

amygdala: one of two small, almond-shaped masses of grey matter that are part of the limbic system and are located deep inside the brain between the temporal lobes of the **cerebral hemispheres**; involved in emotions, emotional learning and memory.

anterior cingulate: is the frontal part of the **cingulate cortex**, which resembles a 'collar' formed around the corpus callosum, the fibrous bridge-like bundle that relays neural signals between the right and left cerebral hemispheres of the brain.

Asperger's syndrome: is one of several autistic spectrum disorders characterised by difficulties in social interaction and by restricted and stereotyped interests and activities. Asperger's syndrome is distinguished from the other ASDs in having no general delay in language or cognitive development. Developmental dyspraxia and atypical use of language are frequently reported.

attention deficit hyperactivity disorder (ADHD): a developmental disorder, largely neurological in nature, affecting about 5 per cent of the world's population. The disorder typically presents itself during childhood, and is characterised by a persistent pattern of inattention and/or hyperactivity, as well as forgetfulness, poor impulse control and distractibility.

auditory stimuli: sound stimuli that may be detected by ear.

autism: a pervasive developmental disorder characterised by a wide range of symptoms, such as severe deficits in social interaction and communication, by an extremely limited range of activities and interests, and often by the presence of repetitive, stereotyped behaviours (also called Kanner's syndrome).

autistic spectrum disorders (ASD): are a spectrum of psychological conditions characterised by widespread abnormalities of social interactions and communication, as well as severely restricted interests and highly repetitive behaviour. The three main forms of ASD are **autism, Asperger's syndrome**, and **pervasive developmental disorder** – not otherwise specified (PDD-NOS).

autobiographical memory: a personal representation of general or specific events and personal facts; it also refers to memory of a person's history.

axon: a long, slender projection of a nerve cell, or neuron, that conducts electrical impulses away from the neuron's cell body (also known as nerve fibre).

basal ganglia: a group of nuclei in the brain interconnected with the cerebral cortex, thalamus and brainstem; basal ganglia are associated with a variety of functions: motor control, **cognition**, emotions and learning.

bipolar: a term used to define things with two (usually opposing) poles.

brainstem: the lower part of the brain, adjoining and structurally continuous with the spinal cord.

Broca's area: an area on the frontal lobe related to the production of speech.

caudate nucleus: a nucleus located within the **basal ganglia** of the brain; originally thought to be involved primarily with control of voluntary movement, now recognised as important for learning and memory.

cerebellum: a region of the brain that plays an important role in the integration of body sensation and motor output. Many neural pathways link the cerebellum with the motor cortex, which sends information to the muscles causing them to move, and the spinocerebellar tract (fibres between the spinal cord and the cerebellum), which provides feedback on the position of the body in space.

cerebrum: the largest and uppermost portion of the brain. The cerebrum consists of two cerebral **hemispheres (cortex)** and accounts for two-thirds of the total weight of the brain.

childhood disintegrative disorder (CDD):   a rare condition characterised by late onset (after three years of age) of developmental delays in language, social function, and motor skills.

cingulate cortex: a prominent part (a ridge of the infolded cerebral **cortex**) found near the middle plane of the brain, above the bridge connecting the two halves. The cingulate gyrus forms part of the **limbic system**, which is associated with mood and emotions.

circle time: refers to any time that a group of people are sitting together for an activity involving everyone; nowadays of wide spread use in schools (also known as group time).

cognition: mind processes which include perception, attention, thinking, memory, language, problem solving, consciousness.

cognitive neuropsychology: aims to understand how the structure and function of the brain relates to specific cognitive processes. Particular emphasis is given to the study of effects of brain injury or neurological illness on mental health with a view to inferring models of how the brain works.

cognitive behavioural therapy (CBT):   is a psychology-based treatment for mental health conditions. Instead of focussing on the past, it concentrates on relearning ways of thinking that lead to more balanced emotions and behaviour.

co-morbidity: the presence of one or more disorders (or diseases) in addition to a primary disease or disorder; or the effect of such additional disorders or diseases.

conduct disorder (CD): a pattern of repetitive behaviour where the rights of others or the social norms are violated.

cortex: a layer of grey matter in the brain that constitutes the layer of the **cerebrum** (cerebral cortex) and is responsible for integrating sensory and motor impulses and for cognitive functions.

corticosteroids: refers to a group of natural steroid hormones, for example cortisol or synthetic drugs.

declarative memory: a type of long-term memory in which we store memories of fact; in addition, declarative memory is divided further into **semantic** and **episodic memories** (for example, the date Isaac Newton was born or the name of the child's first teacher).

dendrite: is the branched projections of a neuron that act to conduct the electrical stimulation received from other neural cells to the cell body of the neuron from which the dendrites project. Electrical stimulation is transmitted onto dendrites by upstream neurons via synapses which are located at various points throughout the dendritic arbor.

developmental coordination disorder (DCD): a term used to describe the difficulties some children experience with movement and postural control, including eye–hand coordination, in the absence of any specific neurological causes such as cerebral palsy (see also **dyspraxia**).

developmental delay syndrome: a general term for developmental disorders such as **dyslexia, dyspraxia, ADD, ADHD, obsessive–compulsive disorder, Tourette's syndrome, Asperger's syndrome** and **autistic spectrum disorders**.

developmental disorders: a term for disorders that occur at some stage in a child's development, often retarding the development. These may include psychological or physical disorders.

dopamine: is a hormone and **neurotransmitter** released by some neurons.

dyscalculia: a term for an impairment of the ability to solve mathematical problems; often linked to a brain disorder.

dysgraphia: a term for an impairment of the ability to write, usually caused by a brain disorder.

dyslexia: a learning disorder marked by impairment of the ability to recognise and comprehend written words.

dyspraxia: a term for an impairment of the ability to execute purposeful, voluntary movement (recently also called **developmental coordination disorder**).

educationally subnormal: subnormal intellectual functioning which originates during the developmental period.

e-learning: learning that is facilitated and supported through the use of information communications technology (ICT) including the internet and intranet.

emotional intelligence: refers to how people relate to others, have social skills and show emotional awareness.

emotional literacy: the ability to be aware of your own and others' emotional states and self-control skills to contain and handle these. The impact of a child's relative emotional maturity or immaturity on their behaviour, performance and personal happiness is being recognised more and more in schools and included in the curriculum.

epilepsy: any of a group of syndromes characterised by transient disturbance of the electrical activity of the brain that may be manifested as some impairment or loss of consciousness, abnormal motor phenomena, psychic or sensory disturbances.

episodic memory: the type of long-term, **declarative memory** in which we store memories of personal experiences that are tied to particular times and places; often linked to eye-witness testimony.

executive control: a central feature control of human actions such as the ability to flexibly adapt to changing situations, realise new intentions, or schedule intended actions; it guides thoughts and behaviour through planning and goal-setting.

foetal alcohol syndrome: a range of birth defects including heart, head and brain abnormalities and mental retardation, occurring in an infant due to excessive alcohol consumption by the mother during pregnancy.

forebrain: is the largest part of the brain, most of which is made up of the **cerebrum**. Other important structures found in the brain include the **thalamus**, the **hypothalamus** and the **limbic system**.

frontal lobe: the largest of five lobes constituting each of the two cerebral hemispheres. The frontal lobe lies beneath the forehead. The frontal lobe significantly influences personality and is associated with the higher mental activities, such as planning, judgment, and conceptualising.

germination area: the area of the brain in which the development of **neurons** starts.

Gilles de la Tourette's syndrome: a neurological disorder characterised by tics – involuntary, rapid, sudden movements or vocalisations that occur repeatedly in the same way.

glial cells: provide support (nutrients and oxygen) and protection (insulate, destroy pathogens and dead neurons) for **neurons**, the other main type of cell in the nervous system.

glucose: simple sugar present in the blood, belongs to chemicals known as carbohydrates. Reactions inside cells involves oxygen and glucose to produce the body's energy.

handicapped (physically):   a child who has a disability of locomotor and neurological orgin which constitutes a disadvandage or restriction in one or more aspects of daily living activities.

hemisphere (cerebral):   one of two sides of the brain addressed either as 'left' or 'right'.

hippocampus: a structure of the **limbic system** that consists mainly of grey matter and has a central role in spatial mapping and memory processes.

hyperlexia: an ability to recognize written words, which is for in advance of being able to comprehend what has been read.

hypersensitive: highly or excessively sensitive.

hyposensitive: less than the normal ability to respond to stimuli.

hypothalamus: a part of the brain that lies below the thalamus regulating bodily temperature and biochemical processes.

labelling: defining or describing a child in terms of his or her behaviour or brain damage. The term also describes the attachment of a mental illness to a person who has been given a specific diagnostic description.

lexical retrieval deficit: the impairment of the retrieval of verbal information from memory.

limbic system: a group of interconnected deep structures of the brain, bordering the **thalamus** and **hypothalamus**, and involved in olfaction, emotion and motivation.

maladjusted: inadequately adjusted to the demands or stresses of daily living.

meningitis: acute inflammation of the meninges, the membranes that cover and protect the brain and spinal cord.

mirror neurons: are neurons that fire both when one acts and when one observes the same action performed by another person.

moderate learning difficulties (MLD):   a general developmental delay. Key features include: short attention span; lack of logical reasoning; immature social and emotional skills; inability to generalise what they learn and apply it to other situations; difficulties with reading and writing, and comprehension; poor understanding of basic mathematical concepts; limited communication skills; underdeveloped coordination skills.

morphology: is a branch of linguistics which studies the phonological structure of the smallest units of speech sounds.

motor cortex: a part of the frontal cortex controlling movement.

multiple intelligences: term originally coined to describe more fully the different and equally important ways of processing the environment.

myelin sheath: the insulating envelope of myelin that surrounds the core of a nerve fibre or **axon** and that facilitates the transmission of nerve impulses.

neurodevelopmental disorders: a fairly new term in medicine and related fields. It refers to a range of difficulties wherein there are gaps, delays or variations in the way a child's brain develops. It can be caused by genetic, environmental, or unspecified reasons, many of which are not yet known. We do know however that these dysfunctions often interfere with learning, behaviour and adaptability across environments. Neurodevelopmental problems may affect one out of every twenty children.

neurological abnormalities: damage to the brain resulting in behavioural deficits.

neuron: specialised cells that make up the body's nervous system. These nerve cells process, store and transmit information from one part of the body to another.

neuronal migration: a process by which neurons travel from their birth place to their final position in the brain.

neurotransmitter: a chemical that is released from a nerve cell which thereby transmits an impulse from a nerve cell to another nerve, muscle, organ, or other tissue. A neurotransmitter is a messenger of nervous information from one cell to another. Often, drugs/medications operate to change the activity or availability of neurotransmitters.

obsessive–compulsive disorder (OCD):   a psychiatric anxiety disorder most commonly characterised by a subject's obsessive, distressing, intrusive thoughts and related compulsions or rituals.

occipital lobe: the rear part, somewhat pyramid-shaped part of each cerebral hemisphere processing visual information.

oppositional defiant disorder (ODD):   a recurring pattern of negative, hostile, disobedient, and defiant behaviour in a child or adolescent, lasting for at least six months with serious violation of the basic rights of others.

orbitofrontal cortex: a region within the frontal lobes, above the eyes, involved in cognitive processes such as decision making emotions, risk taking and suppression of behaviours.

orthography: the study of correct spelling in written language according to established usage.

parietal lobe: The upper middle lobe of each cerebral hemisphere, located above the temporal lobe, processing complex sensory information from the body and movement-related vision; also controls the ability to understand language.

perception: the process by which organisms interpret and organise sensation to produce a meaningful experience of the world. Note: **sensation** usually refers to the immediate, relatively unprocessed result of stimulation of sensory receptors in the eyes, ears, nose, tongue or skin.

pervasive developmental disorders (PDD):   a group of disorders characterised by delays in the development of socialisation and communication skills.

phonology: the study of how sounds are organised and used in natural languages.

phonological disorder: a child does not develop the ability to produce some or all sounds necessary for speech that are normally used at his or her age.

planum temporale: the surface within the temporal lobe of the cerebrum, involved with language.

plasticity: refers to the brain's ability to change and learn consistently.

Polgar sisters: Three Hungarian sisters, Zsuzsa, Zsofia, and Judit Polgar, have achieved chess 'grandmaster' results in their teens, and the youngest Judit, is the highest-ranked player of her age, higher even than Bobby Fischer at a comparable age.

pragmatics: the study of the aspects of meaning and language use that are dependent on the speaker, the addressee and other features of the context of utterance.

prefrontal cortex: part of the frontal lobes nearly above the nose, involved in planning complex cognitives behaviours in the expression of personality and appropriate social behaviour.

pretend play: a prominent ability to represent experience in some kind of thinking. In this complex type of play, children carry out action plans, take on roles, and transform objects as they express their ideas and feelings about the social world.

procedural memory: the long-term memory of skills and procedures, or 'how to' knowledge.

profound and multiple learning difficulties (PMLD):   learners who are likely to have more than one severe disability.

proprioceptive sense: the sense of the position of parts of the body, relative to other neighbouring parts of the body.

resilience: the property of the brain to return some of its structure after deformation that does not exceed its elastic limit. Also used to describe a person's abiity to persevere.

restitution: the act of making good, or compensating for loss, damage, or injury of the brain.

Rett's syndrome: a disorder of the nervous system that leads to developmental reversals, especially in the areas of expressive language and hand use, mainly affects girls.

selective/elective mutism: a psychiatric disorder characterised by a persistent failure to speak in selected settings, which continues for more than one month. These children understand spoken language and have the ability to speak normally.

semantic memory: one of the three types of long-term memory in which we store general world knowledge like facts, ideas, words, problem solving.

semantic-pragmatic disorder: children with this disorder have problems understanding the meaning (semantics) of what other people say, and they do not understand how to use speech appropriately themselves (pragmatics) despite having a fluent, clearly articulated and expressive language themselves.

semantics: the study of relationships between signs and symbols and what they represent.

sensation: the neural synaptic firing of our receptors and the transmission of these firings to the brain. For example, when you touch something, receptors send impulses that travel to the spinal cord and then into the brain for processing and awareness of the stimulation. Sensation normally requires the possibility to become aware. Note that once the stimulation is sent to the brain, is processed further and/or enters awareness, one speaks of perception.

sensitive period: a broad term that applies whenever the effects of experience on the brain are unusually strong during a limited period in development. Sensitive periods are of interest to scientists and educators (for example, Montessori) because they represent periods in development during which certain capacities are readily shaped or altered by experience.

sensorimotor coordination: a system that links sensory information and motor skills, for example vision and prehension or eye–hand coordination.

sensorimotor cortex: an area of the parietal cortex combining sensory and motor functions.

serotonin: a neurotransmitter. It plays a part for example in the regulation of mood, sleep, learning and constriction of blood vessels.

severe learning difficulties (SLD):   learners are likely to have extreme difficulty with reading and writing, and may also require help with face-to-face communication.

somatosensory cortex: the area of the cerebral cortex to which the sensory signals are sent. The somatic senses include vision, hearing, taste, smell and equilibrium.

specific learning difficulties (SpLD):   a difficulty that is specific to a particular area, or that affects a particular process (as distinct from a general learning difficulty, which affects the learning of many different skills) or specific skills.

spindle cells: a specific group of neurons, characterised by a large spindle-shaped cell body, gradually tapering into a single apical fibre in one direction, with only a single fibre facing opposite; appearing late in animal evolution.

synapse: the junction between two neurons or between a **neuron** and a gland or muscle cell. **Neurotransmitters** carry impulses across the tiny gap between the cells.

syntax: the study of the rules whereby words or other elements of sentences are combined to form grammatical structures.

tactile sense/tactile stimuli: a group of senses by which contact with objects gives evidence as to certain of their qualities, as registered by pressure-sensitive sense organs in the skin.

temporal lobe: the lower lateral lobe of either **cerebral hemisphere**, located in front of the **occipital lobe** and containing the sensory centre of hearing in the brain and systems for object recognition and associative learning.

thalamus: a collection of nerve cells deep in the brain. Although it performs many functions, the primary role of the thalamus is to relay sensory information from other parts of the brain to the cerebral cortex.

tics: a habitual spasmodic muscular movement or contraction, usually of the face or extremities.

turn-taking: taking turns is one of the hardest lessons for children under five years to learn. The young child cannot without much experience believe that 'her or his turn' really will come in due time.

vestibular sense: a sensory system located in structures of the inner ear that registers the orientation of the head/body.

visual cortex: part of the brain located in the **occipital lobes** and devoted to processing all aspects of visual input, for example form, colour, size, texture, distance and depth.

visual stimuli: the light rays which elicit a stimulation in the eye, a signal then transmitted to the brain.

visuospatial memory: of or relating to visual perception of spatial relationships among objects which are stored.

Wernicke's area: the area on the **temporal lobe** on the left side of the brain responsible for the comprehension of speech.

working memory: a system for temporarily storing and managing the information required to carry out complex cognitive tasks such as learning, reasoning and comprehension. Working memory is involved in the selection, initiation and termination of information-processing functions, such as encoding, storing and retrieving data.

References and further reading

Alloway, T.P. and Gathercole S.E. (eds) (2006) *Working Memory and Neurodevelopmental Disorders*. Hove: Psychology Press.

American Psychiatric Association (2000) *Diagnostic and Statistical Manual of Mental Disorders – Fourth Edition – Text Revision (DSM-IV-TR)*. Washington, DC: American Psychiatric Press.

Anderson, V. (2002) *Developmental Neuropsychology: A Clinical Approach*. Hove: Psychology Press.

Beaney, J. and Kershaw, P. (2003) *Inclusion in the Primary Classroom*. London: National Autistic Society.

Biel, L. and Perske, N. (2005) *Raising a Sensory Smart Child*. London: Penguin.

Biggs, V. (2005) *Caged in Chaos*. London: Jessica Kingsley.

Bird, R. (2007) *The Dyscalculia Toolkit*. London: Paul Chapman Publishing.

Bishop, D.V.M. (2007) Using mismatch negativity to study central auditory processing in developmental language and literacy impairments: where are we and where should we be going? *Psychological Bulletin* 133: 651–72.

Bishop, D.V.M. and Snowling, M.J. (2004) Developmental dyslexia and specific language impairment: same or different? *Psychological Bulletin* 130: 858–86.

Blakemore-Brown, L. (2002) *Reweaving the Autistic Tapestry: Autism, Asperger's Syndrome and ADHD*. London: Jessica Kingsley.

Blakemore, S.-J. and Frith, U. (2005) *The Learning Brain: Lessons for Education*. Oxford: Blackwell.

Bock, G. and Goode, J. (2003) *Autism: Neural Basis and Treatment Possibilities*. Chichester: Wiley.

Bragdon, A.D. and Gamon, D. (2000) *Brains that Work a Little bit Differently*. San Francisco, CA: Brainwave Books.

Bruner, J. (1997) *The Culture of Education*. Harvard, MA: Harvard University Press.

Butterworth, B. (1999) *The Mathematical Brain*. London: Macmillan.

Butterworth, B. (2005) The development of arithmetical abilities. *Journal of Child Psychology and Psychiatry* 46: 3–18.

Butterworth, B. and Yeo, D. (2004) *Dyscalculia Guidance: Helping Pupils with Specific Learning Difficulties in Maths*. London: NFER-Nelson.

Chiat, S. (2000) *Understanding Children with Language Problems*. Cambridge: Cambridge University Press.

Chinn, S. and Ashcroft, R. (2007) *Mathematics for Dyslexics, Including Dyscalulia*. Chichester: Wiley.

Chomsky, N. (1998) *On Language*. New York: New Press.

Chomsky, N. (2006) *Language and Mind*. Cambridge: Cambridge University Press.

Claxton, G. (2002) *Building Learning Power: Helping Young People Become Better Learners*. Bristol: TLO.

D'Amato, R.C., Janzen, E.F. and Reynolds, C.R. (eds) (2005) *Handbook of School Neuropsychology*. Chicester: Wiley.

D'Amato, R.C., Crepeau-Hobson, F., Huang, L.V. and Geil, M., (2005) Ecological neuropsychology: an alternative to the deficit model for conceptualizing and serving students with learning disabilities. *Neuropsychology Review* 15: 97–103.

Department for Education (1994) *Code of Practice on the Identification and Assessment of Special Educational Needs.* London: HMSO.

Department for Education and Skills (2001) *Special Educational Needs and Disability Act.* Nottingham: DfES Publications.

Department for Education and Skills (2001) *Special Educational Needs code of Practice.* Nottingham: DfES Publications.

Department for Education and Skills (2004) *Removing Barriers to Achievement.* Nottingham: DfES Publications.

Donaldson, M.L. (1995) *Children with Language Impairments.* London: Jessica Kingsley.

Durston, S. (2003) A review of the biological bases of ADHD: what have we learned from imaging studies?. *Mental Retardation and Developmental Disabilities Research Review* 9: 184–95.

Emmons, P.G. and Anderson, L.M. (2005) *Understanding Sensory Dysfunction.* London: Jessica Kingsley.

East, V. and Evans, L. (2004) *At a Glance: A Quick Guide to Children's Special Needs.* Birmingham: Questions Publishing.

Farrell, M. (2004) *Special Educational Needs: A Resource for Practitioners.* London: Paul Chapman Publishing.

Farrell, M. (2006) *Dyslexia and Other Specific Learning Difficulties.* London: Routledge.

Frederickson, N., Dunsmuir, S., Lang, J. and Monsen, J. (2004) Mainstream–special school inclusion partnerships: pupil, parent and teacher perspectives. *International Journal of Inclusive Education* 8: 37–57.

Gaddes, W.H. and Edgell, D. (2001) *Learning Disabilities and Brain Function: A Neuropsychological Approach.* New York: Springer.

Gardner, H. (2000) *Intelligence Reframed: Multiple Intelligences for the 21st Century.* New York: Basic Books.

Gardner, H. (2006) *Five Minds for the Future.* Boston, MA: Harvard Business School Press.

Gathercole, S.E. and Alloway, T.P. (2008) *Working Memory and Learning.* London: Sage Publications.

Goswami, U. (2008) *Cognitive Development: The Learning Brain.* Hove: Psychology Press.

Grandin, T. (1996) *Thinking in Pictures.* New York: Vintage Books.

Griffiths, K. and Haines, J. (2006) *101 Essential Lists for SENCOs.* London: Continuum.

Hanbury, M. (2005) *Autistic Spectrum Disorders.* London: Paul Chapman Publishing.

Hannell, G. (2006) *Identifying Children with Special Needs.* Thousand Oaks: Corwin Press.

Hannell, G. (2007) *Success with Inclusion.* London: Routledge.

Hartas, D. (2005) *Language and Communication Difficulties.* London: Continuum.

Holford. P. (2007) *New Optimum Nutrition for the Mind.* London: Piaktus Books.

Holford, P. and Colson, D. (2006) *Optimum Nutrition for Your Child's Mind.* London: Piaktus Books.

Hull Learning Services (2004) *Supporting Children with Speech and Language Difficulties.* London: David Fulton.

Hull Learning Services (2005) *Supporting Children with Behaviour Difficulties.* London: David Fulton.

Jackson, J. (2004) *Multicoloured Mayhem.* London: Jessica Kingsley.

Jackson, L. (2002) *A User Guide to the GF/CF Diet for Autism, Asperger's Syndrome and AD/HD.* London: Jessica Kingsley.

Joanisse, M.F. and Seidenberg, M.S. (1998) Specific language impairment: a deficit in grammar or processing?. *Trends in Cognitive Sciences* 2: 240–7.

Johnson, M.H. (2005) *Developmental Cognitive Neuroscience* (second edn). Oxford: Blackwell.

Karpov, Y. (2005) *The Neo-Vygotskian Approach to Child Development.* Cambridge: Cambridge University Press.

Kirby, A. (2006) *Mapping SEN.* London: David Fulton.

Knivsberg, A.-M. Reichelt, K.-L. and Nodland, M. (1999) Comorbidity, or coexistence, between dyslexia and attention deficit hyperactivity disorder. *British Journal of Special Education* 26: 42–7.

Kurtz, L.A. (2006) *Visual Perception Problems in Children with AD/HD, Autism and other Learning Disabilities.* London: Jessica Kingsley.

Kurtz, L.A. (2008) *Understanding Motor Skills in Children with Dyspraxia, ADHD, Autism and Other Learning Disabilities.* London: Jessica Kingsley.

Kutscher, M.L. (2005) *Kids in the Syndrome Mix of ADHD, LD, Asperger's, Tourette's, Bipolar, and More!* London: Jessica Kingsley.

Lathe, R. (2006) *Autism, Brain and Environment.* London: Jessica Kingsley.

Leonard, L.B. (2000) *Children with Specific Language Impairment.* London: The MIT Press.

Macintyre, C. (2000) *Dyspraxia in the Early Years.* London: David Fulton.

Martin, D. (2000) *Teaching Children with Speech and Language Difficulties.* London: David Fulton.

Milne, D. (2005) *Teaching the Brain to Read.* Hungerford: SK Publishing.

Mitchell, C. (2005) *Glass Half Empty, Glass Half Full: How Asperger's Syndrome Changed My Life.* London: Paul Chapman Publishing.

Morton, J. (2004) *Understanding Developmental Disorders: A Causal Modelling Approach.* Oxford: Blackwell.

Munden, A. and Arcelus, J. (1999) *The ADHD Handbook.* London: Jessica Kingsley.

O'Brien, J. (1996) *Lightning Learning.* Chicester: The Quantum Group.

O'Regan, F. (2005) *ADHD: the SEN Series.* London: Continuum.

O'Regan, F. (2006) *Can't Learn, Won't Learn, Don't Care: Troubleshooting Challenging Behaviour.* London: Continuum.

Palmer, S. (2006) *Toxic Childhood.* London: Orion.

Palmer, S. (2007) *Detoxing Chidhood.* London: Orion.

Pauc, R. (2006) *Is that My Child?* London: Virgin Books.

Portwood, M. (1999) *Developmental Dyspraxia.* London: David Fulton.

Powell, S. (ed.) (2000) *Helping Children with Autism to Learn.* London: David Fulton.

Prever, M. (2006) *Mental Health in Schools.* London: Paul Chapman Publishing.

Reid, G. (2007) *Motivating Learners in the Classroom.* London: Paul Chapman Publishing.

Rothlisberg, B.A., D'Amato, R.C. and Palencia, B.N. (2003) Assessment of children for intervention planning following traumatic brain injury. In C.R. Reynolds and R.W. Kamphaus, *Handbook of Psychological and Educational Assessment: Intelligence, Aptitude, and Achievement* (second edn). New York: Guilford. pp. 685–706.

Sheridan, S.M. and Gutkin, T.B. (2000) The ecology of school psychology: examining and changing our paradigm for the 21st century. *School Psychology Review* 29: 485–502.

Sheridan, S.M. and D'Amato, R.C. (2004) Partnering to chart our futures: School Psychology Review and School Psychology Quarterly combined issue on the Multisite Conference on the future of school psychology. *School Psychology Review* 33: 1–7.

Smith, A. (2002) *The Brain's Behind It.* Stafford: Network Education Press.

Sousa, D.A. (2001) *How the Special Needs Brain Learns.* Thousand Oaks, CA: Corwin Press.

Spooner, W. (2006) *The SEN Handbook for Trainee Teachers, NQTs and Teaching Assistants.* Abingdon: Routledge.

Stackhouse, J. and Wells, B. (1997) *Children's Speech and Literacy Difficulties.* London: Whurr Publishers.

Stephenson, P. (2007) *Head Case: Treat Yourself to Better Mental Health*. London: Headline Publishing.

Temple, C. (1997) *Developmental Cognitive Neuropsychology*. Hove: Psychology Press.

Thompson, M. (2001) *The Psychology of Dyslexia*. London: Whurr Publishers.

Train, A. (2005) *Attention Deficit Hyperactivity Disorder*. London: Souvenir Press.

Tutt, R. (2007) *Every Child Included*. London: Paul Chapman Publishing.

Tynan, B. (2008) *Make your Child Brilliant*. London: Quadrille.

Ullman, M.T. and Pierpont, E.I. (2005) Specific language impairment is not specific to language: the procedural deficit hypothesis. *Cortex* 41: 399–433.

Warnock, M. (1978) *Report of the Committee of Inquiry into the Education of Handicapped Children and Young People*. London: HMSO.

World Health Organisation (1992) *International Classification of Diseases* (10th revision). Geneva: WHO.

Index

The entries in **bold** type refer to key points for the subject in the book